CLASSIC AIRCRAFT
OF WORLD WAR I

CLASSIC AIRCRAFT OF WORLD WAR I

Melvyn Hiscock

First published in Great Britain in 1994
by Osprey, an imprint of Reed Consumer
Books Limited, Michelin House,
81 Fulham Road, London SW3 6RB and
Auckland, Melbourne, Singapore and Toronto.

ISBN 1 85532 407 5

Editor Tony Holmes
Page design Paul Kime/Ward Peacock
Partnership

Produced by Mandarin Offset
Printed in Hong Kong

Front Cover Cylinders clattering away within the polished metal cowling, Sopwith Pup N5180 cruises over a hazy Surrey after taking off on an early morning air test from Fairoaks airfield. This machine was beautifully restored by the late Desmond St Cyrien in the 1970s

Back cover Propped up on a custom-built tail-wheel assembly, the French Memorial Flight Association's beautifully restored SPAD XIII has the cob webs blown out of its impressive 220 hp Hispano-Suiza rotary engine during a ground run at Le Ferté Alais in the spring of 1993

Title page The Shuttleworth Collection's Avro 504K sits waiting for its turn to display in one of the regular shows held at Old Warden. This is one of the few places where you can hear a rotary-engined aeroplane in Britain, and the Avro 504K, with its 110 hp Le Rhône engine, is a frequent performer

PHOTOGRAPHIC ACKNOWLEDGEMENTS
The editor wishes to thank the following individuals for supplying photographs to illustrate this volume; Dave Davies, Jeremy Flack, Ian Frimston, Howard Levy, Michael O'Leary, Frank Mormillo, Thierry Thomassin, Mike Vines and Richard Winslade

Right The only original World War 1 German aeroplane in flying condition in Britain is the Shuttleworth Collection's LVG C.VI. This two-seat reconnaissance and artillery spotter is powered by a 230 hp Benz BzIV engine, which effectively destroys the pilot's view when on the ground, making the use of groundcrew essential. Here, Chris Morris, Shuttleworth's Chief Engineer, helps to swing the tail around after a display

Contents page Designed to replace the B.E.2, the Royal Aircraft Factory R.E.8 was almost as unpopular as its predecessor! It was just as stable as B.E.2, making evasive flying difficult, it had a tendency to spin if handled carelessly, and would easily catch fire if attacked. It was generally powered by a 150 hp RAF.4a engine, a 6-cylinder development of the earlier RAF.1a, but this example, one of only two survivors, was used postwar by the Belgian Air Force and was powered by a Hispano-Suiza. It is now preserved in the Royal Belgian Army Museum in Brussels alongside several other notable types including a SPAD XIII, Sopwith Camel, Nieuport 23, a Sopwith 'One-and-a-Half Strutter' and a Halberstadt D.IV

For a catalogue of all books published by Osprey Aerospace
please write to:

The Marketing Department, Reed Consumer Books,
1st Floor, Michelin House, 81 Fulham Road, London SW3 6RB

Introduction

There are few circumstances that spur technical development as much as war. It is a terrible fact of life that man is at his most ingenious when called upon to devise more efficient ways of disposing of his fellow man. In aviation terms this is best seen in the advances that took place over the period of World War 2. In Great Britain the threat of war spurred on the development of the Spitfire and Hurricane that replaced the biplane fighters of the thirties. Just a few years later piston-engined aeroplanes were capable of almost 500 mph, and the first jets had entered service. It is less obvious but equally true to say that this also happened during World War 1. Looking back now on the biplanes of the period it is sometimes easy to forget that these frail-looking machines were at the forefront of available technology in the same way that stealth fighters and bombers are today.

In the few short years between 1912, when the aeroplane first went to war, and the armistice in 1918, the aeroplane had changed from being an expensive toy, used by daring young men to impress their peers, to an efficient fighting machine capable of impressive manoeuvrability at relatively high speed up to heights of 25,000 ft.

The pilots, too, had to change. Rather than being a hobby for the rich, aviation became a means of war and the pilot became a soldier who was expected to fight and die, this new concept duly creating heroes and victims. A whole new system of tactics and defences had to be evolved, and a new vocabulary invented and learned.

Today, only a few of these precious machines are maintained in airworthy condition. Others have been built as replicas using the makers' original drawings, when they exist, and original engines and instruments, to recreate types that have long since disappeared. The makers of these aircraft perform such feats of engineering in order that they may experience the flying characteristics of the originals, and so that the general public may get to see, hear and even smell these aeroplanes 'in the flesh'. This replica building and restoration process also enables us to study the basic airframe of these machines, examining the constructional methods to see how they evolved over the war years, and how each of the major participating countries tackled the problems of building faster, stronger and better-armed aeroplanes.

It has been said that the military forces of the world were slow to see the potential of the aeroplane as a weapon of war. This is not entirely true since the military were sponsoring trials of machines as early as 1910, only seven years after the first flight at Kitty Hawk, and only two years after the first successful flights in Europe. At this time aeroplanes were frail, underpowered and unable to stay airborne for any length of time. They needed prepared landing fields and trained pilots, and there was simply no infrastructure in place for either of these things.

The generals and admirals of the major powers were simply too wise to have tied up their resources in a oved weapon that was unproven. Thus, the proving of the aeroplane was left to private pilots with sponsorship from entrepreneurs and companies. In Britain the *Daily Mail* were particularly active in offering prizes for distance and endurance flights, including the prize for the first crossing of the English Channel and, ultimately, the prize for the first crossing of the Atlantic. Louis Bleriot's perilous 37-minute flight from France to Dover on 25 July 1909, and Alcock and Brown's successful Atlantic crossing were just ten years apart, proof of the effect World War 1 had on the development of the aeroplane.

Contents

RFC and RAF

In the years leading up to World War 1 aviation was gradually coming of age. Gas balloons had been used for some time to raise an observer so that he could see further into enemy territory – particularly during the American Civil War – and the use of an aeroplane for a similar role, with the added advantage of it being able to move freely over the area to be inspected, had been tried by several countries.

The problem that the early reconnaissance aeroplanes had was one of durability. The aircraft were frail as a result of them having to be made light enough for the low-powered engines that were available, and they were not able to fly in more than light wind conditions. The Military Aircraft Trials on Salisbury Plain in 1912 were an attempt to bring aviation more up to date. Manufacturers were asked to submit aircraft that could operate in the field in quite arduous conditions, and carry out certain tasks while their performance was measured. One task was the ability to take-off from a ploughed field. It is easy with hindsight to find the criteria measured slightly amusing, but one must remember that the generals in charge of the exercise had as much to learn from it as the manufacturers,

Left There are just five examples of the B.E.2 left in existence, and so when the RAF Museum wanted one they had to build it. The starting point was a rear fuselage that had been in storage for many years. This was sent to the workshops of John McKenzie in Southampton, who built the remainder from the original plans that are still held by the Public Records Office. It is interesting to note that this was McKenzie's first experience in working with wood, and it is safe to say that the quality of workmanship is probably better than any original aeroplane. Even the engine on this B.E.2 is a replica, as with no RAF.1a powerplants available anywhere in the world, the engineers at the RAF workshops at Cardington built this external replica that is indistinguishable from the real thing. Also noticeable here is the lack of ailerons on the wings – early B.E.2s were built with wing-warping instead, thus making moveable flying surfaces redundant

Right Once completed the Museum's B.E.2 was to have been half covered to show the structure underneath, but since the collection already had a Bristol Fighter partially uncovered, it was decided to cover the airframe completely. The markings chosen represent the B.E.2 flown by 2nd Lt W B Rhodes-Moorhouse VC of No 2 Sqn RFC. On 26 April 1915, whilst flying the original B.E.2 number 687, he was sent to bomb the railway station at Courtrai. Although he missed his target with a solitary 100 lb bomb, he rather fortuitously knocked out the line nearby. For this action Rhodes-Moorhouse was posthumously awarded the Victoria Cross, the first for either the RFC or the RNAS in World War 1

and those tasks set were relevant to what the powers-at-be thought might be the situation in a future war. The winner of these trials was built by the American showman, turned pilot and naturalised Englishman, Samuel Cody. His was a massive aeroplane converted from one of his previous designs, and powered by a 120 hp Austro-Daimler engine, it passed all the tests with ease. Two were purchased by the War Office at the end of the trials, but only one was used by the Royal Flying Corps (RFC) and it was soon retired, passing into the care of the Science Museum in London, where it can still be seen today

Many of the aircraft used in the first year of the war were variations on designs that had been seen at the aerial derbys before the war – for example, Bleriots, Farman and Bristol boxkites, Morane monoplanes and the various German Taube, had all flown well before the outbreak of hostilities in August 1914, although a few aircraft were beginning to be designed for the purpose in hand. In the Britain, the Royal Aircraft Factory at Farnborough had begun a series of designs using all of the available technology. However, not all of their aircraft are remembered favourably, a case in point being the Royal Aircraft Factory B.E.2, the 'B.E.' standing for Bleriot Experimental, which simply meant it was a 'tractor' aeroplane, with the propeller pulling the aeroplane along.

It was designed as a two-seat biplane, and was originally powered by an 80 hp Renault engine, although this was later changed to the Royal Aircraft Factory RAF 1a engine, a development of the Renault, which produced 90 hp. As it was to be used as a reconnaissance aircraft, and generally flown

Left The Shuttleworth Collection's Avro 504 was built in 1918 as a rotary-engined 504K, but it was converted to a 504N, powered by a Armstrong Siddeley Lynx, soon after its delivery to the newly established RAF. It was owned at one time by Capt Percival Phillips, a well known barnstorming pilot, whose company, Air Publicity, used it to tow advertising banners. Impressed into RAF service once again during World War 2, the veteran trainer was one of a handful of decidedly geriatric 504s used as glider tugs throughout the conflict. It was discovered in a corner of the old Airspeed factory at Portsmouth Airport in 1951, and restored by Avro apprentices back to its original 504K specs, complete with 110 hp Le Rhône engine. Soon after being put back into the air it was used in the film *Reach for the Sky*, which chartered the chequered career of Sir Douglas Bader. The aircraft is seen here in September 1985 coming into land at Old Warden over the heads of the the people who regularly congregate at the edge of the field to watch the airshow without having to pay! Their financial support would be most welcome to help keep this 'old lady' in the air

by relatively inexperienced pilots, it was built to be stable. The pilot sat in the rear cockpit and the observer up front. As the latter's cockpit was surrounded by the struts and bracing wires of the centre-section, his view was somewhat limited, and when a machine gun was fitted to later versions, he had an equally restricted field of fire if he was not to pepper his own aircraft. It would have been more convenient to have swapped the cockpits around, but it is easier to design an aircraft so that the pilot sits in the back, with his disposable load – in this case his observer – nearer the centre of gravity. Later aircraft such as the Bristol Fighter and the D.H.4 were designed with the pilot in front partly as a result of lessons learned with the B.E.2, and they were never flown without an observer/gunner, or a similar weight of ballast, in the back seat.

The B.E.2 was also widely criticised for being too stable. If attacked it was very difficult to manoeuvre, and the type earned the nickname of 'Fokker Fodder'. Once again this was not entirely the B.E.2's fault for it had been designed before the war as purely an observation platform, and it was generally similar in layout and capability to other aircraft of the 1913-era. The B.E.2's problem was not that it was such a bad aeroplane, but that it was kept in service and production for far too long – late production B.E.2es were still being produced in 1918!

Other manufacturers were also busy developing specifically military aeroplanes. Among these were some which were to become almost household names. The Bristol Aircraft Company produced the Scout, a small and fast single-seater, which initially was armed with just the pilot's

Right The earliest surviving original Avro 504 is now owned by Kermit Weeks. This was built as a 504J in 1916 but, like many others, was converted to 504K specification. It usually flies with a radial engine, although it can easily be converted back to rotary power if required. The 504 is relatively easy to fly for an aeroplane of this period, but can be tricky to land since it has a very narrow-track undercarriage. To prevent the wings being damaged on landing, its is fitted with hoops under the lower wingtips, and the long skid beneath the undercarriage stops the aeroplane nosing over and damaging the propeller – a feature that was no doubt put to use many times during the types' long and distinguished career as a training aeroplane

own hand weapons, and A. V. Roe of Manchester produced what was to become one of the finest aircraft in history, the Avro 504. The 504 was ordered by both the Admiralty and the War Office for use with the Royal Naval Air Service (RNAS) and the Royal Flying Corps (RFC) respectively. It was strong and light and initially powered by a 80 hp Gnôme engine. Its operational highpoint came in November 1914 when three 504s, each armed with four 20 lb bombs, attacked the Zeppelin sheds at Friedrichshafen. Direct hits were scored on the shed which contained a fully inflated Zeppelin, and this was destroyed in the ensuing fire. Later 504s were used as night fighters in the defence of London, but it was as a training aeroplane, most notably with the School of Special Flying at Gosport, in Hampshire, and as a postwar barnstormer, that it became best known.

While in service it was flown with just about every engine available; Clerget, Le Rhône and Gnôme rotaries, A.B.C. and Armstrong Siddeley radials and even in-line engines. Its final military operations were performed in 1940 when several of the later 504N models, powered by an Armstrong Siddeley Lynx engine, were used as glider tugs.

As the war progressed, it became clear that any one side was going to try to prevent its enemy from undertaking reconnaissance flights by shooting at the aircraft engaged in carrying out such missions, either by anti-aircraft guns (known during World War 1 as Ack-Ack after the phonetic alphabet 'A' of the time), or by shooting at them from other aircraft. The side that controlled the sky could make as many reconnaissance flights as they wished. This was a lesson that was learned early, forgotten once or twice in

Above During the late 1970s the Leisure Sport company commissioned a number of replica aeroplanes for display at their theme park in Surrey. Some of these were static only, built for a World War 1 airfield set in the park, but others were built as flyers. This D.H.2 was constructed by Vivien Bellamy at Land's End airfield in Cornwall, and it was built following the company's decision to have a pusher aeroplane as part of their display. As the only known surviving factory drawings of the D.H.2 are two general arrangement views, Bellamy had to virtually redesign the aeroplane, powering it with a 120 hp Le Blond radial engine. Following Leisure Sport's decision to sell off the machines during the 1980s, the D.H.2 was employed briefly in a period film, before passing to Brian Woodford, who has a collection of de Havilland aircraft, and whose father flew D.H.2s during World War 1

Right The Royal Aircraft Factory F.E.8 (the 'F.E .' standing for 'Farman Experimental, referring to its pusher layout) was externally similar to the D.H.2, and was the last single-seat pusher fighter in service with the RFC. Building a replica of the F.E.8 was an easier job for New Yorker Cole Palen than building a D.H.2, since almost all of the drawings for the former have survived. Palen's replica is powered by a Le Rhône rotary and regularly flew at Old Rheinbeck airfield. Following Palen's untimely death in 1994 a trust has been formed to continue to operate what was one of the first, and finest, collections in the USA in memory of a man who did a great deal to bring old aeroplanes to people's attention

history, and demonstrated to obvious effect during the Gulf War of 1991.

In order to successfully prevent the opposing side's aircraft from going about their daily work it was necessary to mount guns on those machines allocated to do the 'preventing'. Early fighters, or scouts as they were known, used the pilot's own small arms. This was ineffective since the guns were inaccurate when used in this way, and a single hit from a 9 mm or .303 bullet could easily pass right through the fabric skin of the aircraft being attacked, resulting in only a fabric patch having to then be doped onto the hole by a diligent airframe fitter back at the aerodrome to return the aeroplane to its former glory. Hitting a vital piece of aircraft or pilot was unlikely as each aviator tried to manoeuvre his aeroplane into a firing position. Clearly the more ammunition one could fire at the other chap the more chances one had of the odd bullet actually hitting something which might be important. The answer was to fit machine guns onto the aircraft.

A machine gun is generally a quite heavy piece of equipment which is likely to adversely affect the performance of the aircraft it is fitted to. It is also quite cumbersome to aim, especially if fitted to an aeroplane which is busy trying to dodge bullets fired from an opponent. As more powerful engines were becoming available and designers were learning the tricks of their trade, aircraft could be built bigger and stronger, enabling them to carry the extra weight of the gun – aiming the weapon was a little less straightforward, however.

One way to fly an aircraft and to aim a machine gun at the same time is to

Left Despite their shortcomings, pusher aeroplanes did afford the pilot excellent forward visibility. The arrival of reliable interrupter gear meant that pilots were placed behind the engine and wings once again, both of which impeded their vision. Geoffrey de Havilland, chief designer of the Aircraft Manufacturing Company (AIRCO) at Hendon, designed his D.H.5 so that the pilot would be in front of the leading edge of the upper wing. In order to do this, and keep the centre of gravity in the right place, he had to backstagger the wings by almost two feet. This improved forward visibility at the expense of rearward visibility, and since many attacks came from the rear this was not a popular choice amongst pilots. The D.H.5 was eventually relegated to the ground-attack role, where it was used with some success. This replica, built in the 1980s by John Baptist Shively of Florida, differs from the original in having a steel tube fuselage and a 150 hp Lycoming engine. It is seen here over Lake Guntersville, Alabama, piloted by its present owner, Frank Ryder, who runs the nearby Guntersville Replica Fighter Museum

Right The simple designation Sopwith 'LCT' stood for Land, Clerget, Tractor, and this neatly summed the aeroplane up as, a) not a seaplane, b) powered by a Clerget rotary and c) fitted with a propeller at the front. However, like many Sopwith aeroplanes, it will forever be remembered by its nickname, the 'One-and-a-Half-Strutter'. This was derived from the unusual arrangement of the centre section struts, caused by joining the upper wing panels together, rather than having them attached to a separate centre section. The 'Strutter was one of the more successful aeroplanes of World War 1, being used by the RFC and RNAS as a general reconnaissance aircraft, light bomber and even as a single-seat fighter. It was also built in France under licence, and used by the Americans and Russians. The RAF Museum's example, shown here, is a replica built by Viv Bellamy for Leisure Sport, and finished at about the time they decided to sell their aircraft. Consequently, this flew appropriately for just one-and-a-half hours (or one hour per strut), before being retired into Hendon

have a specific member of the crew responsible solely for each task. This not only makes the aircraft even heavier, but introduces the problem of how the two men work together to bring the guns to bear on the enemy. Clearly it is simpler to use just a pilot to aim a gun attached to an aircraft, and to make his task even easier, to have the gun pointing forwards so that all he has to do is aim the whole aeroplane at the target. The problem here was that machine guns of the period were very prone to stoppages, and needed constant attention from the pilot. Therefore, they could not be placed out of his reach on the wings, for eaxample, as was the case on many World War 2 aeroplanes.

Secondly, they could not fire through the propeller arc without removing the blades in the process, so designers either had to offset the guns and train the pilot to shoot at an angle, or build aircraft with pusher engines, thus giving the pilot a clear view ahead. The British used a number of pusher designs including the Vickers Gunbus, the Royal Aircraft Factory F.E.2 two-seater and F.E.8 single-seater, and the AIRCO D.H.2, designed by the young Geoffrey de Havilland, who went on to build the famous Moth series of light aircraft , the Comet racer which won the England to Australia race in 1934, the Mosquito fighter-bomber of World War 2 and the world's first all jet transport, the Comet airliner.

Pusher designs were a temporary success, but they were generally slower than similarly powered conventionally-configured designs due to the drag caused by the many struts and wires needed to hold the tail to the rest of the airframe. They also left the pilot somewhat exposed as, in the event of a

crash, he was among the first parts of the aircraft to reach terra firma, and would often be crushed as the engine behind him broke free from the airframe. He was also exposed during air fighting. The best way to attack was directly from the front, and he had no engine block ahead of him to deflect any bullets.

Elsewhere others were turning their thought to the same problem. Roland Garros, the great prewar French pilot who had been first to cross

Above The Sopwith Pup, so-named because it resembled a small 'Strutter, is known in Sopwith Company documents as the 80 hp Le Rhône Scout. With its combination of light weight and generous wing area, it was very pleasant to fly, and several original airframes and replicas have existed over the years. The Shuttleworth collection's Pup was actually completed as a Sopwith Dove, the postwar two-seater development of the Pup, and was converted back to full military specification some years ago. It now flies in the colours of No 3 Wing RNAS, and is a regular performer at the air pageants held at Old Warden throughout the summer

Right Since the early retirement of Viv Bellamy's 'Strutter, one has had to travel to America to see a flying example. Javier Arango was photographed here piloting his Warner Scarab-powered 'Strutter replica in company with Chuck Wentworth in his Fokker Dr.1 replica and Merlin Call in Javier's SE.5a replica. Javier evidently likes old aeroplanes since he also has replicas of the 'Stutter's little brother the Sopwith Pup, a Fokker D.VII and a Pfalz D.III

Left In the mid-1960s a retired naval officer, Desmond St Cyrien, discovered the remains of two Pups, a Camel and many spare parts in a barn in Lincolnshire. After acquiring the find lock, stock and barrel, he set about rebuilding the first of the Pups, and this was duly finished by the early 1970s. On 30 June 1974 he took the Pup to Old Warden to fly alongside the Shuttleworth Collection's example, and the pair are seen here heading towards the crowd – St Cyrien's machine is being capably flown by the late Neil Williams, whilst Sqn Ldr 'Dickie' Martin is at the controls of N5180. Desmond St Cyrien later sold the Pup to Doug Arnold, the well-known collector of warbirds, and he in turn swapped it with the RAF Museum for a Spitfire, thus giving the RAF Museum a largely original Sopwith Pup, but grounding the aeroplane forever

the Mediterranean in a Morane H monoplane, fitted the propeller of his Morane N with steel deflector plates so that any bullet hitting the airscrew would be knocked away. He used this ingenious invention to great effect and many other Morane Ns, including some used by the British, were also fitted with the plates. The heyday of this method was short lived, however, as Garros was forced down in enemy territory and his modified aircraft captured by the Germans. His radically altered propeller was closely inspected, and the Dutch aircraft designer Anthony Fokker, who was working for the Germans, was asked to come up with a similar installation for one of his own aircraft.

He went one stage further by following up a prewar design that had been largely ignored – synchronisation. By linking the firing of the gun with the passing propeller blades through a simple interrupter gear, he showed that bullets could pass through the arc of the prop without touching it. The prototype installation was fitted to a new monoplane that Fokker had designed which was based loosely on the Morane H. This was a simple aircraft with a welded-steel tube fuselage and wooden wings. It was powered by a 80 hp Oberursel rotary engine, which was a copy of the French Gnôme, and was fitted with a single machine gun in front of the pilot.

The aeroplane was demonstrated to the Imperial German Army High Command by Fokker himself, and legend has it that he was ordered to the front to shoot down an Allied aircraft to prove the system. Whether this is true is debatable, but the new Fokker was a success with the pilots at the

Right The simple, but pleasing, lines of the Pup are seen to advantage in this earlier shot of the Shuttleworth Pup taken during its time as N5180. Despite only boasting and engine of 80 hp, the Pup climbed and turned well due to its ultra-light weight, and it could out perform contemporary German aircraft. It was also surprisingly rugged despite its diminutive size. Pups were used by both the RFC and the RNAS on land and at sea, and as many as 800 were still on charge at the time of the Armistice since few aircraft could match its performance at altitude

front, and it was ordered into production immediately. The main production version, the E.III, was fitted with a 100 hp Oberursel UI rotary, but was otherwise very similar to the prototype. The new aircraft began to make its mark on the fighting immediately. It was relatively manoeuvrable and was soon shooting down a considerable number of the less nimble, and less effectively armed, aircraft of both the British and the French.

As with all developments in war it was not long before the Allies had also developed an effective synchronisation method of their own, and several aircraft emerged during 1916 that were to become classics of the period.

The Sopwith company, based in Kingston-upon-Thames, designed a single-seat scout aircraft for the RNAS. This was an attractive biplane powered by an 80 hp Le Rhône engine and fitted with a single Vickers gun ahead of the pilot. Although never named officially, it became known as the Sopwith Pup. It was a very manoeuvrable and rugged biplane which became an instant success, and many former RFC and RNAS pilots have been quoted as saying the Pup was the nicest aircraft of the period in terms of its general flying characteristics. It also had the ability to reach high altitudes – with its large wing area it would still be manoeuvrable when other aircraft of both sides were struggling to keep their composure in the thin air. Even after the type had been superseded at the front by later designs, Pups were still used as top cover for large raids over enemy territory.

In France the Nieuport company produced the Nieuport 17. This was a larger and more powerful version of their earlier Nieuport XI Bébé, and was powered by a 110 hp Le Rhône rotary engine. It entered service with the RNAS and the RFC, as well as with the French, in the summer of 1916. This was a popular aircraft as it was manoeuvrable and had an excellent rate of climb. Many were also armed with a Lewis gun on a mounting above the centre of the upper wing, which could be lowered in flight in order to change the ammunition drum, but could also be fired from this depressed position.

Albert Ball, the renowned British ace, would stalk the enemy in his favourite Nieuport 17 from below their rear-quarter, thus keeping in their blind spot. When underneath he would fire upwards into the unsuspecting victim, many of whom were downed before they had fired a shot in return. This idea was also used during World War 2 when German nightfighters were fitted with upward firing 20 mm cannon, known as *Schräge Muzik*, which accounted for many unsuspecting RAF heavy bombers.

Another French design which was to prove very successful was the SPAD VII. Unlike many of the aircraft used by the Allies, this machine was powered by a water-cooled Hispano-Suiza V8 engine of 150 hp. The extra weight of the engine meant that the SPAD had to be heavier, but it was very strong and could be dived at considerable speed. It too was used by the RNAS and RFC as well as the French, and was to remain in service until the end of the war, serving alongside its replacement, the SPAD XIII.

The pace of development on both sides was furious. The Fokker monoplane was soon outclassed by its new opponents and its replacements at the front included the first of the new Albatros biplanes, the D.II. The Albatros designer, Robert Thelen, dispensed with the more common rotary engine and decided to use the larger and heavier Mercedes six-cylinder water cooled in-line engine of 160 hp. To help overcome the weight disadvantage of the engine, he designed an aerodynamically clean aircraft with a semi-monocoque plywood fuselage, rather than the wire-braced and fabric covered wooden structure favoured elsewhere. Since the plywood skin carried some of the in-flight loads placed on the fighter when airborne it was a very strong machine, and with its engine partially enclosed in the fuselage, created much less drag than many of its contemporaries.

The Albatros D.II was also designed to carry twin machine guns, Thelen's theory being that a heavier armed and faster aeroplane would win over the lighter and more manoeuvrable French and British designs by sheer brute force, and the effect that the new design had over the Western Front confirmed this point. Among those to use the new fighter was Oswald Boelke, perhaps the most far-seeing aerial tactician of World War 1, and Manfred von Richthofen, destined to become known as 'The Red Baron', who used his Albatross D.II to shoot down Major Lanoe Hawker VC, a leading RFC ace of the period who was flying a D.H.2.

Above right Following the sale of Desmond St Cyrien's first Pup, the second was also rebuilt, although it was not completed until a decade later. By this stage Sir Thomas Sopwith had become interested in the project, and before final completion of the airframe, St Cyrien had him sign the fin, and his signature can just be seen above the Company logo. This Pup remains in airworthy condition at the Museum of Army Flying at Middle Wallop, in Hampshire, and is flown very occasionally. Perhaps its finest hour came when it was part of the flypast over Sir Thomas Sopwith's house on the occasion of his 100th birthday, but it has also flown in formation with a British Aerospace Harrier at a Biggin Hill airshow, and was present at the 80th anniversary of the RFC at Netheravon in April 1992, although high winds prevented the Pup from flying on this occasion

Below right The Museum of Army Flying's Sopwith Pup is flown for no more than an hour or two each year, and then only when the conditions are perfect. There can be few better places to fly an old aeroplane than its home of Middle Wallop, which boasts the largest grass airfield in Europe. As a result of the base's overwhelming size, take-offs and landings into wind are always possible, and despite being an extremely active airfield, it is almost unused in the evenings when the wind is light and the Pup is at its happiest flying

Left Rotary-engined aircraft are interesting to operate, as the fuel and air mixture is fed into the crankcase and literally thrown into the cylinder by centrifugal force. On this 80 hp Le Rhône fitted to the Shuttleworth Collection's Sopwith Pup, the mixture travels up the brass pipes on the outside of the engine. The engine operates on a total loss oil system basis, using Castor Oil which is liberally thrown into the slipstream and back along the aeroplane by the exhaust, the exit for which is through the open exhaust valve in the top of each cylinder. The neat cowl over the 80 hp Le Rhône serves a dual purpose, for not only does it direct cooling air over the cylinders, but it also acts as a collector ring for the oil, most of which drains out of the underside, rather than being sprayed over the unfortunate pilot. The cowl also prevents the exhaust flames from setting fire to the rest of the aircraft. Many World War 1 pilots would drink liberal quantities of Brandy to overcome the unfortunate effects of the castor oil, which always escaped despite the presence of the cowling

One of the most influential aircraft of the time was another product of the Sopwith Company, who produced a new fighter for the Admiralty for use by RNAS squadrons. This was a triplane design powered by a 130 hp Clerget rotary engine, but which was still only armed with a single gun. The new aeroplane had a remarkable rate of climb and was very manoeuvrable. It was not long before one was forced down on the German side of the lines, and it had a remarkable effect on those who saw it.

Literally days after the Triplane's fortuitous arrival on German soil, several firms were invited to submit designs for official Army testing. Among these was a aircraft from Anthony Fokker. After his Eindekker monoplanes had been replaced at the front, Fokker was unable to come up with a design that could match those of the Albatros, Halberstadt and Pfalz companies, and he had also lost his chief designer, Martin Kreutzer, in a crash in 1916. The Dutchman had duly replaced him with Kreutzer's assistant, Rheihold Platz, who had been a welder with Fokker since 1912. Platz was untrained, but he had learned well and had a natural talent. He was to remain Fokker's chief designer for almost 20 years, but was not acknowledged as such as Fokker himself liked to claim that he personally

Right The Clerget engine was a more developed powerplant, featuring dual ignition and better control of the inlet and exhaust valves through the use of dual push rods, rather than the single push/pull rod on the Le Rhône. The 130 hp version shown here was the standard engine on Sopwith Triplanes, and was also used on many Sopwith Camels. The unusual brown colour of this engine is due to the accumulation of several years' worth of burnt castor oil which may look unsightly, but can protect the working parts from corrosion

designed his own aircraft.

The triplane that Platz put together was to become one of the most famous aircraft of the period, even though only a relatively small number were ever built. Instead of using the braced wooden structure of the Sopwith, Platz designed his triplane with a welded steel tube fuselage, following established Fokker practice. This was braced internally with piano wire, and the aircraft was powered by a 110 hp Oberursel rotary. The wings also differed from the Sopwith – whereas the latter's wing had been built up around two spars, the Fokker Triplane was built around a single double-box spar that was immensely strong. It meant that the Fokker had to have a thicker wing, but this gave more lift, even though it increased drag. However, the strength of the wing meant that no external bracing was needed, and so the drag-producing bracing wires were dispensed with.

The first triplane was also built without any struts between the wings, but production versions were fitted with them to stop the wings from fluttering. Platz even designed the undercarriage to provide lift, enclosing the axle with a wing-like fairing. The Fokker Dr.1 was, like the Albatros, fitted with twin machine guns. The new design was an instant success, and

Above left The rotary engine contains some of the finest engineering of the period. Each cylinder is machined from a solid drop-forged ingot, and each cooling fin is thin enough to cut a careless hand. The front plate, which included the propeller shaft, was also a single-piece on this 80 hp Le Rhône, although some other makes used a two-piece plate. The engines were relatively expensive due to them being hand-built

Below left The single Vickers gun of the Sopwith Pup is seen here on the Fleet Air Arm Museum's replica N6452, built in the early 1980s for collector Guy Black. Behind the gun is the tiny windshield, complete with its padded surround, that was intended to give the pilot a modicum of protection in the event of a crash landing. Also visible are the twin holes for the oil tank and petrol tank filler caps just behind the engine, and the staining of the fabric caused by the ever-present Castor Oil. On the side of the fuselage on the metal panel behind the cowling is an access panel for the carburettor and magneto, and behind that is the inlet pipe for the engine air

Right Some idea of the forward view from a Pup can be gained from this view of the Shuttleworth Collection's example. With the tail down, forward visibility is limited, and having the gun and windshield in the way doesn't help matters a whole lot either

Above The Fleet Air Arm Museum's Pup has had some interesting times. Completed as the first of a pair in 1983, it was offered for sale at a Christie's auction at Duxford that same year. It was flown to the auction venue from its temporary base of Old Warden, but a magneto problem en route resulted in the pilot having to perform a perfectly safe forced-landing about five miles short of its destination. Rather than dismantle the aeroplane, it was decided to tow it to Duxford, and the Police agreed to close the main Royston to Cambridge road so that the Pup could finish its journey. Following the auction it was bought by Soho entrepreneur Paul Raymond, who was planning to open a war museum in a disused theatre in Whitehall. The Pup spent a few months suspended from the roof with a motor turning its engine, before being sold on when the museum project eventually foundered. Acquired for a very reasonable price by the Fleet Air Arm Museum, it is kept in airworthy condition at Yeovilton

Left From time to time the Pup is flown, usually by Robin Bowes, whose more usual mount is a Fokker Triplane replica, and it is seen here in company with the museum's Sopwith Camel replica. The Pup wears a typical RNAS scheme, with a natural linen fuselage and camouflaged wings representing the many Pups that served with the Navy. It was in one such Pup that Sqn Cdr E H Dunning, RN, made the first deck landing on a moving ship on 2 August 1917. Sadly, Dunning was killed a few days later when, attempting a similiar recovery at sea, his engine cut after he decided to go around to make another approach

Left Starting a rotary engine can be a bit of a ritual. Each cylinder needs top be primed with neat petrol from a syringe, which is squirted into the exhaust valve as the engine is turned over by hand. One of the masters of the craft was the late Wally Berry, who looked after the rotary engines at Old Warden for over 30 years. He is seen here pulling through the Le Rhône of the Collection's Pup, whilst being assisted by Chief Engineer Chris Morris

Below There are very few venues in the world where you can see several genuine World War 1 aeroplanes flying. Old Warden is one such place, and this line up includes their Sopwith Pup, LVG C.VI and Bristol Fighter, as well as the D.H.51, the forerunner of the Moth family, and a direct descendant of the B.E.2

Above This earlier photo of a similar line up shows the same three aircraft, together with the collection's Hawker Tomtit. With careful maintenance and strict limiting of the hours, and indeed minutes, flown by these aircraft, there is no reason why they should not fly for many years to come

Right Javier Arango has been flying since the age of eight, and he has notched up a considerable amount of hours, many of which have been achieved in his impressive collection of World War 1 replicas. He is seen here flying his Sopwith Pup replica

of the first three built, one was used for static testing, one went to Manfred von Richthofen (serial 102/17) and one to Werner Voss (103/17). Voss took to his instantly, and used it up until his death in September 1917. It says much that in his final fight with SE.5as of the RFC's No 56 Sqn, Voss was totally outnumbered, yet he fought for several minutes, and managed to put holes in all of the attacking aircraft.

Richthofen took to his more cautiously, using his older Albatros D.Va in turn, although he did score his 60th air victory on his first combat flight in the Dr.1. Richthofen's 102/17 was lost on 15 September 1917 when being flown by Lt Kurt Wolff, and the 'Baron' himself was killed in April 1918 whilst flying Dr.1 serial 452/17. Despite its postwar fame, mostly due to the Richthofen connection, the Dr.1 was not as common as has been suggested.

A total of 320 Fokker Dr.1s were built, and only some 171 were ever to be found at the frontline at any one time, with these machines being persistently dogged by wing failures caused by faulty manufacture. For a while the aircraft were even grounded while replacement wing panels were made and fitted to the aircraft at the front. By early 1918 faster and equally as manoeuvrable fighters were coming into service, and the Dr.1 was relegated to secondary operations and training.

Among those aircraft coming into service were several that were to achieve equal fame to the Triplane. In France the SPAD XIII was beginning

Above Of the 152 Sopwith Triplanes built, only two are known to have survived – one in the RAF Museum and another in the Soviet Air Force Museum at Monino, near Moscow. The Northern Aeroplane Workshop's project to create a perfect replica for the Shuttleworth Collection came to fruition in 1990. This reproduction is about as perfect as it is possible to get. So much so that on seeing the work being carried out, Sir Thomas Sopwith allowed the group to use the next Triplane construction number – 153 – making this a 'late production' original aeroplane! Engine problems delayed the first flight, but it is seen here being run up by Shuttleworth's chief pilot, John Lewis, after the gremlins had been eradicated

Above The 130 hp Clerget engine on the Northern Aeroplane Workshop's Triplane proved to be a little difficult to get to run smoothly, and it was not until 10 April 1992 that the Triplane finally took to the air. A plug lead problem caused the flight to finish after just 11 minutes, but in that time John Lewis was able to report that the Triplane climbed very well at 80 mph indicated, and stalled at 50 mph on approach power. He also reported that the ailerons and elevators were good, but that the rudder was 'like pushing through mud'. It was 3 May before the Triplane flew again, and this photograph shows the fighter at rest after that second flight

to reach frontline squadrons. This was a larger version of the SPAD VII, powered by the 220 hp Hispano-Suiza engine and armed with twin Vickers guns. Although it was dogged with problems, due to the unreliability of the engine – particularly those from certain sub-contractors – the SPAD XIII was a great success. It was very fast, and although not as manoeuvrable as some other frontline types, including the SPAD VII, was used to great effect by both the French and the American squadrons that were forming in France by early 1918.

A variation of the SPAD XIII was the SPAD XII, a few of which were built in early 1917. It was built at the suggestion of the French ace, George Guynemer, who appreciated the need for heavier firepower than was available from one or two machine guns. He persuaded the SPAD company to fit a 37 mm cannon between the cylinder blocks of the aircraft's Hispano-Suiza engine so that it fired through a hollow propeller hub. The rate of fire was very slow, but the effect of the cannon shells on the target were devastating. The type was not used much due to its relative lack of manoeuvrability, and the fact that the cannon needed to be reloaded by hand after each shot, but it was nevertheless the forerunner of the heavily armed aircraft of World War 2.

Meanwhile, in Britain the Royal Aircraft Factory was busy producing the SE.5a. This too had the Hispano-Suiza engine, or a developed version built

Left Following the first flight there were only a few weeks left before the Triplane was scheduled to make its public debut at the Shuttleworth *Military Aviation 92* show, scheduled for June 7. Flight testing was finished just two days before the event, but this did not leave enough time to get the relevant paperwork back from the Civil Aviation Authority – the Triplane therefore remained grounded until the following show. Photographed here on one such test on 16 May, John Lewis can be seen discussing the aircraft's progress with the late Wally Berry

by Wolseley, and was armed with two machine guns – a Vickers firing through the propeller and a Lewis gun mounted on the top wing. The SE.5a was reputed to be the fastest fighter at the front, and was also so strong that it could be dived at speed without fear of it shedding its wings. SE.5as were to remain in service after the war, and many were also sent to the United States, where they were used by the Army Air Service for a number of years. Some of these also eventually found their way into the early Hollywood epics such as *Wings* and *Hells Angels*.

The Bristol Company, whose Scout had been one of the first true fighters, produced the F.2B, or Bristol Fighter. This was unusual since it was a two-seater, the gunner in the rear cockpit having a Lewis gun mounted on a Scarff ring, and the pilot having a single Vickers gun firing through the propeller. Initial operations with the new aircraft were a disaster – on 5 April 1917 six Bristol Fighters were attacked by the pilots of Manfred von Richthofen's *Jasta* 11, who rapidly shot down four of their number.

The main problem initially experienced with the new Bristol was that pilots attempted to fly the aircraft so that the gunner in the rear cockpit could get a shot at the attacking aircraft. It was soon realised this was tactically unsound, so the Bristol Fighter was eventually used in the same way as any other fighter, with the pilot trying to bring his own gun to bear on the attacking aircraft, while the gunner covered his tail and did his best to deter attacks from the rear. When used in this way the F.2B was a formidable fighting machine. With its Rolls-Royce Falcon III V12 engine it was fast and, despite its size, was quite manoeuvrable. It is sad to relate that in World War 2 this lesson was forgotten when the Air Ministry specified the Bolton Paul Defiant, which had only rear-firing armament in the form of a powered-turret behind the pilot. The Defiant had no forward firing guns, and so was severely limited as it had to fly in exactly the same way as the early Bristol Fighters, suffering high casualties as a result.

Without a doubt, one of the finest fighters produced by Britain during World War 1 was the Sopwith Camel. Again, this was not an official name, but one bestowed upon the aeroplane due to the metal fairing, or 'hump', that covered the breeches of the guns. The Camel was designed so that all of the major structural weight such as the engine, fuel, pilot and guns, were as close to the centre of gravity as possible. This meant that it was finely balanced and very manoeuvrable. The Camel was produced for both the RFC and the RNAS, as well as being supplied to some American squadrons. It was powered by a variety of engines, including the 110 hp Le Rhône and the 130 hp Clerget, whilst some of the RNAS Camels were even powered by the Bentley rotary of 150 hp.

With its relatively powerful engine, small frame and all the weights concentrated near the centre of gravity, the Camel could be lethal for an

Below left All Triplanes on the Western Front were flown by the RNAS. The most well-known of these belonged to No 10 Wing (commanded by Raymond Collishaw), whose noses were painted black. Reflecting this sombre decor, each aircraft was given an approrpiate name such as *Black Maria*, *Black Prince* and even *Black Death*. Equally distinctive, and perhaps less well known, were the Triplanes of No 8 Wing, and the Shuttleworth aircraft is painted to represent N6290 *Dixie II* of 'Naval 8'

inexperienced pilot, but in the hands of an expert it could out turn any other fighter at the front. It was so nimble that it was possible to loop it straight after take-off, although this wasn't the most sensible of manoeuvres! Many pilots found it to be the ideal fighter, and the Camel accounted for more enemy aircraft than any other World War 1 fighter.

French designers, too, were producing some superlative aircraft. The entry into service of SPAD XIII was delayed by its engine problems, and the Nieuport company decided to stick with the rotary engine to produce its rival Type 28. Unlike earlier Nieuport designs, which had a sesquiplane

Above Among the replica's built for Leisure Sport was this static Triplane, representing Collishaw's own *Black Maria*. He was to finish the war as the highest scoring Allied pilot to survive the conflict, with 63 confirmed victories. Static replicas at a theme park might not be everyone's idea of 'the real thing', but if they inspire someone to look a little deeper into the subject then they are not a waste of time

Right Although the Triplane missed being able to take part in the June 1992 show at Old Warden, it was able to make a further test flight in the morning before the display, where it was caught by the camera of Mike Vines. Clearly visible in this view is the wire linking all three ailerons, plus the small propeller-driven 'Rotherham' pump on the cabane strut in front of the pilot that pressurised the main fuel tank. The quality of this reproduction is clear to see, the result of 19 years hard work, and a lot of solid research

layout with the lower wing being much smaller in area than the top wing, the Nieuport 28 was a true biplane. Powered by the 160 hp Gnôme monosoupape rotary, it was a streamlined and purposeful looking fighter armed with twin Vickers machine guns.

The French, having by then almost solved their chronic engine problems, decided to standardise on the SPAD series of aircraft since they were faster, and as a result only a few Nieuport 28s were used by the *Aviation Militaire*. Many Nieuport 28s were transferred to the United States Air Service, however, where they were flown by four squadrons, and some were taken back to America after the war. Another aeroplane that was overshadowed by the SPAD was the Morane AI, known in service as either the Morane XXVII, when fitted with one machine gun, or the XXIX when fitted with two. This was a parasol monoplane fighter that boasted superb handling qualities, although it was hamstrung by its relatively 'breathless', and at best temperamental, 150 hp Gnôme monosoupape rotary engine. Although its frontline career was short-lived, the AI found a home with many training squadrons due to its good flying characteristics – these units often replaced the Gnôme engine with the more reliable Clerget of 130 hp.

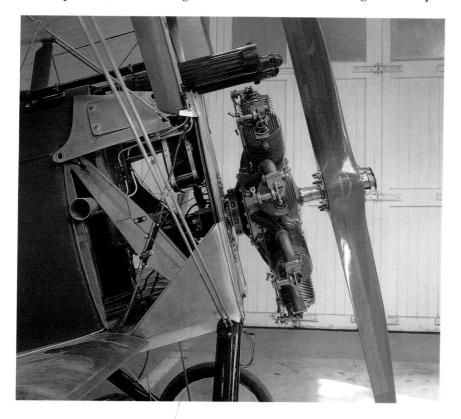

Left The third of Desmond St Cyrien's cache of Sopwiths, and the last to be rebuilt, was Sopwith Camel B6291. This machine was restored over a period of several years, before finally being finished in 1989. For a while the Camel was exhibited at the Museum of Army Flying, but was unable to fly due to the lack of a suitable powerplant. Shortly before his death in 1992, St Cyrien sold the Camel to Tony Ditheridge, whose company, AJD Engineering, has produced some impressive replica aircraft and rebuilds over the years. Tony moved the Camel to Old Warden and fitted a 110 hp Le Rhône, since a 130 hp Clerget – the type originally fitted to this particular Camel – was unavailable. Visible here are the inlet pipes on the 110 hp Le Rhône that run from the back of the engine, the pushrod-operated exhaust valves, the wooden engine bearer and the air inlet pipe behind it

Right The small size of the 110 hp Le Rhône is evident from this photo of Chris Morris fitting the engine to the Camel. Behind the engine can be seen the long inlet pipe that fed the fuel and air mixture into the crankcase. Also clearly visible here is the 'hump' over the gun breeches that gave the aeroplane its nickname. B6291 was built by the Sopwith Aviation Company at the Ham works, near Richmond, Surrey, as part of a batch from B6201 to B6450, and it was most probably test flown at Brooklands. The first of the batch came off the line in August 1917, and B6291 was completed during September of that same year. It was sent to France but was badly damaged in a crash landing after only a few days. Sent back to England for repair, it served out the rest of the war in a variety of training squadrons. After the Armistice it was part of an assorted batch of aircraft that were bought by two former RFC officers for a barnstorming team. This venture foundered through lack of funds, and the Camel ended up in the Lincolnshire barn

Whereas the SPAD tended to overshadow other French aeroplanes, the next Fokker design did much the same to many other German fighters in the last year of the war. After his return to favour with the Triplane, Fokker designed two more projects for the Air Service. The first of these, which became known as the D.VI, was a biplane powered by a 110 hp Oberursel rotary. The other was a larger biplane powered by the 160 hp Mercedes water-cooled six-cylinder in-line engine, and was designated D.VII. The argument as to which World War 1 fighter was the best at its dedicated role of aerial domination will no doubt continue forever, but the D.VII will always finish somewhere near the top of any list.

It was strong and powerful, and fitted with twin machine guns. Relatively easy to fly, it was said that a D.VII could turn an average pilot into a good one, and frontline operators were quick to see the potential of the aircraft, and other good designs like the Pfalz D.XI and later Halberstadts were passed quickly by as pilots sought out D.VIIs. Even maintenance crews preferred the D.VII, as the Pfalz D.XI, for example, was a two-bay biplane with a relatively complex structure that required careful rigging. The D.VII, on the other hand, had cantilever wings that required no bracing wires, the flying surfaces being simply bolted to the fuselage. The interplane struts made assembly of the aircraft very straightforward, which was an absolute boon for the Germans as the Air Service often moved its units by rail. The D.VII received its highest accolade in the Armistice agreement, which stated that all machines of this specific type should be surrendered – this was the only aircraft to be mentioned by name. Fokker, however, had other ideas, and smuggled a large number of completed and part-completed airframes and engines out of Germany to his native Holland, where he began his business again.

The D.VII was not Fokker's last design of the war, however, he and Platz continuing to experiment with different configurations into the summer of 1918. Their final design was a parasol monoplane powered by the 110 hp Oberursel. A very 'clean' fighter overall, its strong wing was mounted on a fuselage that was similar to the Triplane. The D.VIII was initially known as the E.V, or Fokker's fifth monoplane, and early versions were plagued with wing failures caused by his now-infamous lack of quality control. After the type had been withdrawn from the front for several months in 1918, new wings were built and the aeroplane re-introduced as the D.VIII, which was not technically correct since the D usually denoted *Doppeldekker*, or biplane, and the E, *Eindekker*, or monoplane.

Just as fighter aircraft developed out of types that were designed for general duties, so too did aircraft designed for other specific jobs such as bombing and reconnaissance. In the early years of the war, artillery observation was done by aircraft such as the B.E.2, which would observe the fall of shells and then fly back over the command post, dropping a message bag detailing the adjustments needed for better accuracy. Clearly this was a time consuming method, and experiments were soon underway to fit a radio to the aircraft so that the results could be transmitted back to the command post without having to leave the area under attack. Early radios, and the batteries needed to power them, were both heavy and unreliable in the testing conditions of the frontline, and these trials were not altogether successful, although by war's end many aircraft on both sides were fitted with radios, the German LVG C.VI being one such type.

Photography also played a major part in the aerial war. Missions of this type were initially performed by holding the camera over the side of the aircraft's fuselage and taking a picture of whatever appeared below. By the end of the war, newer cameras that gave a much clearer picture were available, and some aircraft were adapted for this role. The Breguet 14.A2

Right Some of the early restoration work on St Cyrien's Camel was done by British Aerospace in the same building in which it was constructed many years before. Sir Thomas Sopwith was very interested in the rebuild, and it is said that he arranged for a number of brand new Camel parts to be searched for and dug out of the Kingston factory store, which were incorporated in the aeroplane. Its second 'first' flight was on 27 July 1993 at Old Warden, and the paperwork was completed speedily enough to allow it to take part in the show on 1 August. Piloted by Stuart Goldspink, the Camel flew in the display in company with the collection's Pup, and once again after the show to allow Mike Vines to photograph it

on display in the *Musée de l'Air* at Le Bourget, Paris, had sliding panels under the fuselage to allow the internally-fitted cameras to get an unobstructed view of the ground below.

Early attempts at bombing were also somewhat haphazard. In order to carry any bombs many early aircraft had to dispense with the services of the second crew member, and those bombs which could be carried were generally not big enough to cause any serious damage. The handful of successful raids that were flown invariably relied more on luck than judgment to inflict any telling damage on the enemy. As the war progressed the importance of tactical bombing – the destruction of targets of tactical importance behind the enemy's lines – was appreciated by both sides, and aircraft were developed that could carry a modest amount of bombs such as the F.E.2, the D.H.4 and the French Voisin.

It was also realised that bombers were afforded an extra degree of protection if operated at night, which resulted in a whole new system of flying having to be learnt. The Germans were quick to realise the importance of bombing, and their Gotha twin-engined bombers could not only harass the frontlines, but were also perfectly capable of crossing the channel and bombing London. To counter this the capital was ringed with night defence squadrons that initially used obsolete aircraft such as the Avro 504 as a nightfighter, but which were eventually equipped with Sopwith Pups, Camels and SE.5as as the attacks increased.

The Allies also realised that a larger aircraft, powered by big water-cooled engines, could carry enough fuel and bombs to reach targets inside

Right Despite its small size, some Camels were converted into two-seater trainers although, as far as is known, none were fitted with a rear gunner's position. Since this child is, thankfully, unarmed, the pilot of the Fleet Air Arm Museum's Warner-powered Camel replica may have decided that he needs an extra pair of eyes watching the tail of his aeroplane, or it could just be that they start them very young in the Navy

Germany. The most notable of these were the Handley Page 0/100 and 0/400. These were large biplanes with a span of 100 ft and an endurance of eight-and-a-half hours, which gave them a range of almost 800 miles, with reserves, and they could carry a disposable load of 3500 lbs in addition to their fuel. Handley Page also built examples of the V/1500 four-engined bomber that had a range of 1350 miles with a bomb load of one ton. This mammoth aeroplane would have been able to reach Berlin, but the war ended before it could be used.

Another aeroplane that narrowly missed hostilities, but which duly found its place in history, was the Vickers Vimy. Only one example actually reached France before the Armistice was signed, but another, flown by Capt John Alcock DSC and Lt Arthur Whitten Brown, made the first non-stop crossing of the Atlantic in 1919. The Vimy was to remain in service with the RAF for many years, a transport derivative of the classic bomber still be used by several auxiliary units in 1939!

From its early beginnings when frail aircraft attempting to undertake duties for which they were often not designed, military aviation during World War 1 grew to incorporate many of the tasks and tactics still used today. The rapid development of fighter aircraft was proof that each side realised that those who controlled the skies could affect what happened on the ground. Many of the tactics developed by Boelke, and advocated by von Richthofen, are still relevant today, and the use of tactical bombers during the last 18 months of World War 1 was a prelude to the terrible destruction wrought from the air by both sides during World War 2.

Above At one time Leisure Sport had a truly impressive collection of replica fighters. Among these were two Sopwith Camel built by Viv Bellamy, one of these was completed with a 130 hp Clerget rotary, and can be seen today in the Brooklands Museum on the site of the old race track and airfield; the scene of many Camel test flights. The other was built with a Warner engine, and this eventually found its way to the Fleet Air Arm Museum, who repainted it in the colours of No 3 Wing, RNAS. The Camel was maintained in airworthy condition for a while, but the expense of operating a replica aircraft has kept it grounded for sometime now, and it is presently exhibited fitted with a non-airworthy Clerget engine

Left Skysport Engineering in Bedfordshire, have built and rebuilt a number of aircraft over the last few years. Among them was this Sopwith Dove replica for British collector Roger Reeves. There are few differences between the Dove and the Pup – the fuselage is deeper, the wing tips squarer, the fin slightly different and the wing stagger changed to allow for the movement in the centre of gravity. Despite these superficial alterations, this aircraft is undeniably related to the Pup

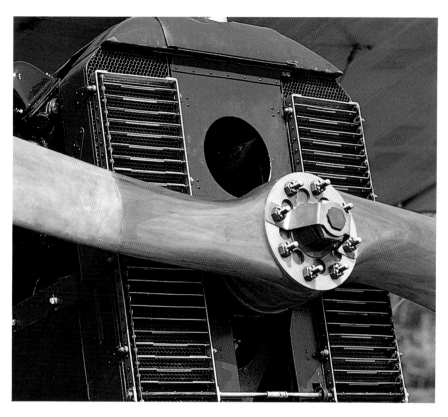

Above The Royal Aircraft Factory S.E.5a was unusual for a British aircraft as it used the Hispano-Suiza V8 engine, or the British variation, the Wolesley Viper. This gave the aeroplane a blunter nose than the rotary-engined Sopwiths as the radiator was kept behind the propeller to make the most of the flow of air to cool the water. The radiator was also fitted with shutters to vary the amount of air being allowed over the engine. These are clearly visible in this photo of the Shuttleworth Collection's S.E.5a, as is the right hand bank of cylinders of the Wolesley Viper engine

Right The Dove was designed to be an affordable postwar light aircraft, but failed to find a market. Whether this was due to its price, or the fact that it was too early onto the market, is hard to tell, but the lightplane business was finally cornered a few years later by another World War 1 aircraft designer, Geoffrey de Havilland, whose Moth series of aircraft were similar in size to the Dove, had an almost identical airfoil section and were powered by a cut down Renault engine, as previously used on the B.E.2. This Dove is currently based at Old Warden where, for a short time in 1993, it was possible to see a Pup, Camel, Triplane and Dove, all of which were airworthy

Right Until recently there were two airworthy S.E.5as in Britain – the Shuttleworth Collection's S.E.5a and the S.E.5e belonging to the estate of the late Patrick Lindsay. The S.E.5e was built in England as an 'a', but was rebuilt in the United States by the Eberhard Steel Company, hence its new designation. The United States Army Air Corps (USAAC) used the S.E.5e for a number of years, and following their eventual retirement found their way into the Hollywood epics of the 1930s. The Lindsay S.E.5e was no exception, and it was flown in at least two major films when owned by the legendary Hollywood pilot, Frank Tallman. After his death it found its way into the Wings and Wheels collection in Orlando, Florida. At the auction following the demise of the collection it was acquired by Patrick Lindsay, who had it totally rebuilt by Personal Plane Services as an S.E.5a, and finished in the colours of the RFC's leading ace, Edwin 'Mick' Mannock, of No 56 Sqn. On rare occasions the two S.E.5as could be seen together, but sadly this is unlikely to ever occur again as the aeroplane has been sold back to an American collector

Above The Shuttleworth Collection's S.E.5a is one of several that were used during the 1920s by a company called Savage Skywriting. These were fitted with longer exhausts and smoke generating equipment, and used to write advertisements in the air. Three of these aircraft have survived – 'F904' with the Shuttleworth Collection; 'F938' with the RAF Museum; and G-EBIB with the Science Museum in London, the latter having recently been converted back to its skywriting configuration. Of these, only the Shuttleworth example has remained airworthy

Left Mannock's distinctive markings can be clearly seen as Tony Bianchi, whose company rebuilt the aeroplane, taxies back to his parking space following his display at Old Warden. This aeroplane may not have had a distinguished wartime history, but when in service with the USAAC its pilots have included none other than Charles Lindbergh and Gen Charles 'Chuck' Yeager, which must surely make it unique

Above In this view of the S.E.5a being readied for flight, the overwing Lewis gun can be clearly seen, as can the telescopic gunsight in front of the pilot. These gunsights were particularly prized by the Germans, and many salvaged examples were used on their fighter aircraft of the period

Right The Shuttleworth Collection's S.E.5a was rebuilt in the late 1950s at the Royal Aircraft Establishment at Farnborough, where it had been designed, and was based there for a while after the rebuild. During this time it was often flown by the Officer Commanding Farnborough, Wg Cdr Dave Bywater. He can be seen here formating on the Shuttleworth Collection's D.H.51 for the camera of Dave Davies on a photo sortie over Old Warden. Such flights are both rare and short due to the limited engine life of the aircraft, and are usually combined with some sort of air test or training sortie

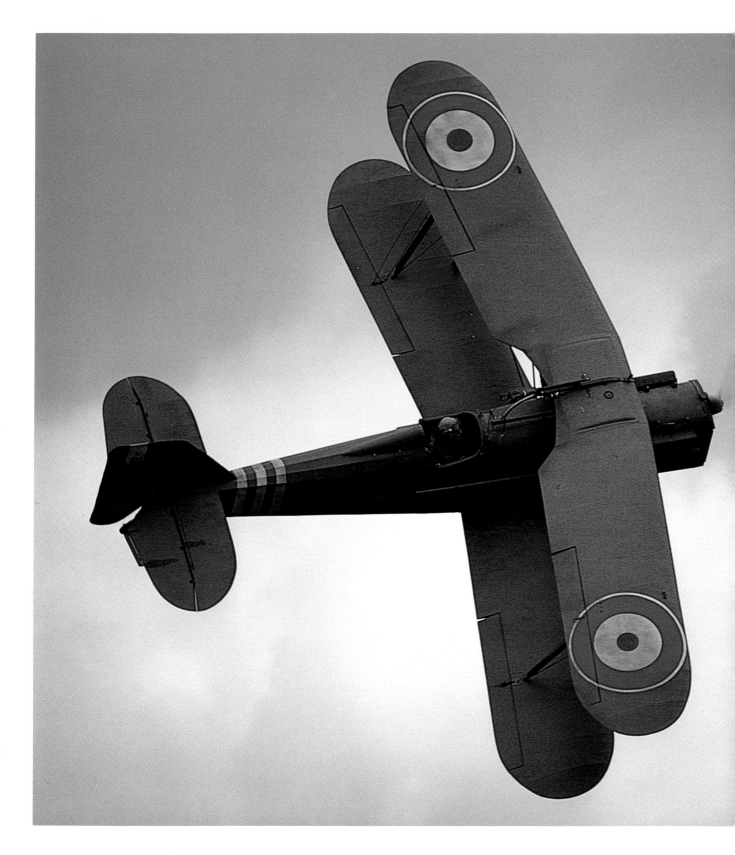

Above Fortunately, the plans for the S.E.5a have survived reasonably intact, and it is possible to build replica aircraft. Finding the correct engine, however, is another story, and many fly with more modern powerplants. Javier Arango's S.E.5a replica is no exception, having a 200 hp Lycoming 0-360. This is much easier to maintain than the Hispano-Suiza of the original, and allows the pilot to fly more often than would be the case if the original engine was fitted. Although purists might scoff, this does allow many people who would not normally see World War 1 aeroplanes to get some idea of what these fighters were like, and allows owners such as Arango to fly more than a few hours per year

Left It is not just private individuals who build replicas. For a film company involved in the making of a World War 1 epic, serviceability and reliability are more important than historical accuracy. Many aircraft used in films over the years have been conversions of familiar types. As far back as 1930, Howard Hughes' *Hells Angels* used the Travelair 4000 as a substitute Fokker D.VII, and the Stampe has been a favourite for portraying a number of differing types. Among these is the S.E.5a, several of which were converted for the wonderfully realistic 1976 epic, *Aces High*, by Personal Plane Services. New cowlings were made, guns were fitted, tail surfaces reworked and the fuselage altered for a single cockpit. During the filming the 'S.E.5as' flew for about 30 hours, considerably longer than most original aeroplanes manage in five years!

Above The Bristol Fighter was one of the finest aircraft to emerge from World War 1, and it continued in RAF service until 1932. The Shuttleworth example was built in 1918, but saw no wartime service. It was bought from the government in 1936 by a former RFC officer who planned to restore it, but this came to nothing. In 1949 it was discovered in a barn and acquired by the Shuttleworth Trust. They passed it to the Bristol Aeroplane Company, who had built it 31 years before, for restoration. It first flew again in 1951 in the hands of Bristol's chief test pilot, Bill Pegg, and for many years flew in the No 208 Sqn scheme of silver dope that it wore whilst serving with the unit in Turkey in 1923

Right In order to shoot down an opponent during World War 1 it was advisable to get onto his tail, where he was most vulnerable since his guns fired forwards. The Bristol Fighter changed all of this as it had a purpose-built 'sting in the tail' in the form of a Lewis gun and gunner, whose life literally depended on him beating off any attacking aircraft. The Scarff ring onto which the Lewis gun was fitted was easy to move and lock into position, and allowed the gunner to fully devote his energies into firing the gun, rather than supporting it

Above The Bristol Fighter's Rolls-Royce Falcon engine is like most other World War 1 powerplants in that it lacks a starter motor. Among the items found with the Bristol was a Hucks Starter, a Model T Ford chassis fitted with a clever device for turning the engine over to start it. However, this is not always available, so the engine is then started by the 'Armstong' method. Most rotary engines can be started by one man, but the massive Falcon needs two or three with their arms linked to turn over the compression. An added advantage of having more than one man pulling is that the individual at the 'business end' nearest the propeller, is pulled clear by the others, thus making it less likely that he will come into painful contact with the propeller once the engine has fired

Above right Once the engine is turning, the checks are made quickly to preserve valuable engine hours and to keep the temperatures within limits. With no brakes, run-ups are made against chocks, with the added security of a man on each wing. These men will also assist the pilot to taxy since the aeroplane is difficult to steer on the ground, and visibility is hampered by the massive engine cowling stretching some way in front of the cockpit. This view also shows the empty gunner's position, which must be ballasted to compensate for the missing crewman

Right One of the highlights of the summer are the evening shows held at Old Warden once a month from May through to August. They start at 7pm and carry on until almost dark. One advantage of this time is that the wind is often much lighter, allowing the more fragile aircraft to fly. Although the Bristol hardly qualifies as fragile, it does benefit from the evening light which brings out the colour of the camouflage. Following a rebuild in the early 1980s, the Bristol Fighter was repainted in the standard PC10 scheme of 1918 so as to allow it to represent the many F.2Bs that served during World War 1

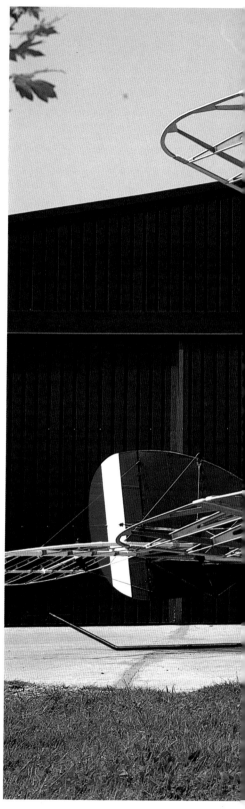

Right For many years there were just two Bristol Fighters in the Britain – the Shuttleworth example and E2581 in the Imperial War Museum collection. The discovery of six original fuselage frames being used as roof trusses in a barn at Weston-on-the-Green changed all of that, however. One of these was used by the RAF Museum, who built new wings, a very convincing dummy engine and a lot of original parts to make the F.2B they now have on display at Hendon. Another was rebuilt with a Hispano-Suiza engine, and is now in the Brussels Air Museum, whilst a third went to Aero Vintage in Sussex, who are rebuilding it to fly. This one was also rebuilt to fly for collector Stephen Grey, using an original set of wings that were discovered in storage. Ian Frimston's photo shows the uncovered aeroplane being rigged in June 1992

Above Once covered, Grey's Bristol Fighter was painted in the markings of D8084 of No 139 Sqn on the Italian front, but its completion has been delayed for several years due to the difficulty of finding an engine. Very few Rolls-Royce Falcon engines are known to exist, and a worldwide search eventually found one in Prague. This is now at Duxford being rebuilt, where it will eventually be fitted to the completed airframe so that it can fly in 1995

Aviation Militare

Hand in hand with developments in aerodynamics and aircraft design was the development of ever-more powerful engines. The powerplants used in early wartime aircraft were pretty much the same as those that had been used before the conflict had started, and for the most part they were heavy, underpowered and unreliable. The search for engines with enough power to get an aircraft off the ground, whilst still being light enough not to render this fundamental aspect of 'flying' impossible, had been the main problem facing mechanical engineers of the late nineteenth and early twentieth centuries. It has often been said, and is probably quite true, that if Otto Lilienthal, the German pioneer who flew hang-gliders in the 1890s, had been able to find a lightweight engine he would have beaten the Wright Brothers to the honour of the first powered, and sustained, flight by several years. Sadly, he was killed in a gliding accident before he could unite his designs with a suitable powerplant.

In the years leading up to World War 1 the two best known engines were the Antionette, a beautifully made water-cooled V8 engine that developed 50 hp, and the similarly-rated Gnôme rotary, a five-cylinder radial engine that rotated with the propeller. The basic idea behind a rotary engine is that if the cooling air is not passing across the engine at a sufficient speed, it can be helped by also moving the engine itself. This was achieved by fixing the crankshaft of the engine to the airframe, and fixing the propeller to the crankcase. The whole engine would then turn, taking the propeller with it. The obvious advantage was that with the engine spinning there was plenty of air rushing past it to cool it sufficiently.

The equally obvious disadvantage was that getting a petrol and oil mixture to the cylinders was complicated by the fact the engine was not in the same place for more than a split-second. This was solved by injecting the mixture through the hollow crankshaft to a butterfly valve inside, where a mixture was released into the crankcase. This was then thrown by centrifugal force into the cylinders. For the engine to be effective, it had to be light in weight, which made it ideal for use in aircraft, but it was complicated and expensive to manufacture.

Many of the best fighter aircraft of the period were fitted with rotary engines of differing powers and styles. The three main types were all French – the Gnôme, Le Rhône and Clerget – although others were built. For example, the German Oberursel rotaries were copies of either a Gnôme or a Le Rhône, depending on the engine type, and the excellent and quite

Above right The Blériot XI of cross-channel fame was a very successful aeroplane, but was prone to wing failure. Blériot's answer was to beef up the airframe with larger spars and fit two seats. In this form it was known as the Blériot XI-2, or *Militaire*, and examples were used by both the French and British in the early years of the war. These were powered by a variety of engines, although this replica, built for the Salis Collection, is powered by an 80 hp Le Rhône. It is painted in the markings of Adolphe Pégoud, Blériot's former test pilot, who was killed in action during 1915

Right The Caudron G.III was used by both the French and the British as an observation aircraft early in the war, and a large number eventually found their way into training establishments. They could be powered by either a rotary engine or by a 100 hp Anzani radial powerplant. Several original examples survive, and a handful of replicas have also been built, in this case by the Salis Collection at La Ferté Alais, near Paris, which was powered by a 100 hp Anzani. Sadly this G.III is no longer flying, having been traded with a foreign museum

Above Originally built for the film, *The Blue Max*, Personal Plane Service's Morane N replica has since been used in a number of World War 1 movies. The airframe has been adapted from the original plans to make it more reliable and safer for film work. The fuselage is made from welded steel tube, and the wings have been adapted to take ailerons rather than be warped. Tail surfaces were also altered since the originals had no separate elevators – they simply pivoted about their spar, which made the Morane more than a little unstable in pitch. The aeroplane is powered by a Continental C90 in place of the 80 hp Le Rhône of the original, and the end result is an aeroplane that looks sufficiently original for film work, yet is suitable for flying for longer than a few minutes

Left The G.III is so identifiable with the Salis Collection – the old airfield sign even featured a drawing of one – that it was only a matter of time before a replacement aeroplane was built. Started in 1992, the new replica is powered by a 120 hp Walther radial, and first flew early in 1994. The Caudron is relatively crude, with warping wings and the lower tail booms doubling as tail skids. It is also extremely slow due to its relatively huge size, and the amount of drag produced by the structure advanced Bentley was a redesign of the Clerget. Many of the engines were built by sub-contractors in England, the United States and Italy. Their use in fighters was due to their light weight and compact size, which enabled a small and manoeuvrable aeroplane to be built around them. The downside of this was that they were very thirsty for both fuel and oil, and needed far more attention than radial or in-line engines. There was also a limit as to how much power could be extracted from them, their rotation setting a limit on how fast they could run, and therefore the power available. The Bentley B.R.2, which was undoubtedly the finest engine of the period, was fitted to the ultimate Sopwith fighter, the Snipe, and was rated at 230 hp. Over the ensuing decades since World War 1, engineers have re-appraised the final rotary designs of the conflict and come to the conclusion that engines such as the big Le Rhônes and Gnôme Monosoupape 9Ns were somewhat underrated. An example of the latter powerplant, which was rated at 160 hp, was fitted to Aero Vintage's restored Nieuport 28, and its owner reported that it would pull the aeroplane into a near vertical climb – he also reckons that its power output is somewhere nearer to 400 hp!

Rotaries are notoriously difficult to operate, however, and usually run at either idle or full speed, with fine control being next to impossible to achieve. In order to give some measure of control in approach, for example, a switch (known as the 'blip switch') was fitted to the control column. This would cut the ignition to several or all of the cylinders, giving a brief drop in power. Nieuport took this one stage further, with the engine being controlled by switching off the ignition of several of the cylinders. This switch panel had several settings which would allow all the cylinders, or combinations of them, to fire. It is possible to run the 160 hp Gnôme on just one cylinder, which then sounds like a series of guns firing. As an indication of how powerful these engines are, the Nieuport 28 flew for the first time with its ignition selector switch in position three, which meant that only every second cylinder was firing.

When weight and size was not a problem, or when sheer brute power was needed, designers turned to in-line, or V-shaped, engines. As stated, the pre-war Antoinette would produce 50 hp from its eight cylinders. By the end of the war the Liberty engine, a V12 built in America, was rated at 400 hp, and the W-configured Napier Lion was just coming into service rated at 450 hp. Both of these engines were used for many years after the war, and Rolls-Royce were working on their 600 hp Condor engine, which provided a lot of valuable experience used later in the design of the Merlin and Griffon engines of World War 2, just as the Armistice was declared.

Many German and Austro-Hungarian aircraft were powered by six-cylinder in-line engines varying from the Argus of 100 hp to the Mercedes of 260 hp. The Fokker D.VII was originally built with the Mercedes engine of 165 hp, but later versions, known as the D.VIIF, were fitted with the

Above right Like the Sopwith Pup, the Nieuport XI was a light, agile, fighter powered by a 80 hp Le Rhône engine and armed with a single machine gun. Unlike the Pup, it did not feature an interrupter gear, so the gun had to be mounted so that it fired outside the propeller arc. The only original Nieuport XI is in the *Musée de l'Air* at Le Bourget, but several replicas have been built for film work and private collections. This one, seen at La Ferté Alais in 1977, was one of several built by Williams Flugzeugwerke, run by expatriate American Art Williams, in Germany, for a film that never made it into production

Below right Like many film replica's, the construction of the Williams Nieuport XI was simplified. In this case the 80 hp Le Rhône has been substituted by a small radial engine, and the fuselage appears to be made of steel tube rather than the braced wooden structure of the original. The small rods protruding from the fuselage ahead of the first set of struts are the aileron actuating rods which operate the ailerons, via a torque tube behind the upper wing rear spar

increased compression BMW IIIa of 185 hp. This was designed for operation at high-altitude, and could not be flown below 6000 ft on full throttle. It did, however, give the D.VII very good top ceiling performance, which combined with its thick wing to make it difficult to beat at height.

The 1919 edition of *Janes All the Worlds Aircraft* refers to the Hispano-Suiza engine, as used in the S.E.5a, SPAD, Sopwith Dolphin and many other Allied combat aircraft of the period, as being 'One of the most successful engines in the World'. Although the company was Spanish, the engines were built under licence in England, France, Czechoslovakia, and the US and many were still earning their keep years after the war had ended. Not all versions of this remarkable V8 were as good as others though. The 180 hp ungeared version, as fitted to the SPAD VII, was a fine engine and very reliable for its time. The 220 hp version developed from it, on the other hand, was used in the SPAD XIII and was nowhere near as

Above Film companies are not always driven by accuracy when portraying World War 1 aeroplanes. This Nieuport XI fuselage was converted to take a single wing, and was actually flown in this configuration at La Ferté Alais some years ago! Whether it was intended to represent a Morane Parasol is unclear, and it was nicknamed 'The Bastard'

Above Another of the Salis collection's replicas that has since gone into a museum is this Deperdussin A type racer. The original was conceived by Louis Bechereau, who went on to design SPADs, and it was the first aircraft to exceed 200 kmph. It was powered by a 160 hp Gnôme rotary that was faired into the monocoque fuselage

Right The overall lines of the Deperdussin are surprisingly modern for a machine built so long ago, and it is perhaps surprising it was not developed into a fighter. Construction, too, was advanced, with the fuselage being a monocoque plywood structure. The replica differs from the original only in having a more modern 160 hp Gnôme engine, and ailerons instead of a warped wing

successsful, at least early on. Whilst this engine was similar to the 180 hp version, considerable problems were encountered with the reduction gear. There were also difficulties with some of the sub-contractors building the engines, whose quality control was less than perfect. The Brasier Company in France was notorious for making bad engines, and they are reported to have said at the time, 'It is better to have bad engines than no engines at all'! The reduction gears they made on engines fitted to SPAD XIIIs would frequently fail, leaving the propeller to rip itself free of the aeroplane, often taking the radiator with it. Since the SPAD was already tail heavy, this reduction in weight at the forward extremity of the aeroplane would cause it to fall out of the sky tail first, usually resulting in the pilot's death.

By the end of the war, the cooling problems that had prompted designers to build rotary engines were all but solved. This paved the way for larger air-cooled radial engines. Some radials were used during the war, but many, the Canton Unne used in Salmson bombers and some Voisins for example, were water-cooled. In England the A.B.C. Company were building air-cooled radial engines by the end of the war, but these were prone to vibration and failure. The Snipe, for example was to have had an A.B.C. Dragonfly of 320 hp, but was built with the Bentley rotary instead. The Bristol Aircraft Company was also experimenting with air-cooled radials and by 1918 the first of these, named the Cosmos Jupiter, had appeared. This was the forerunner of a series of engines bearing the Bristol name that were to continue right up to the 1950s.

Above The first of Nieuport's aircraft to feature the familiar sesquiplane layout and V-shaped struts was the Nieuport X two-seater of 1914. This was powered by an 80 hp Le Rhône engine, and was armed with whatever was available to the observer! This particular example is an original aircraft that was taken to the United States by the legendary French ace Charles Nungesser to publicise a film in 1925. It was restored in 1988 and wears Nungesser's coffin and candles insignia in memory of its former owner

Above right One of the finest restorations of recent years has been the SPAD XIII of the Memorial Flight Association, who are now based at Dugny, close to Le Bourget. The SPAD is an original aircraft that was a partial gift to the association from Jean Salis. Through the group's close links with the *Musée de l'Air*, original parts were acquired, and an original 220 hp Hispano-Suiza installed. By 1988, when Thierry Thomassin took this photo, the fuselage was ready for covering. About 75 per cent of the fuselage wood and about 90 per cent of the metal pieces are original, thus making this SPAD one of the most highly prized of all surviving World War 1 types

Right The SPAD cockpit is typical of the period, with instruments installed almost at random. Visible in this view is the petrol filler pipe running down from the right hand side to the fuel tank beneath the floor, the hand-cranked starting magneto on the lower right side, and the back end of the engine, which comes almost back to the pilots knees, and provides his feet with a constant stream of warm air!

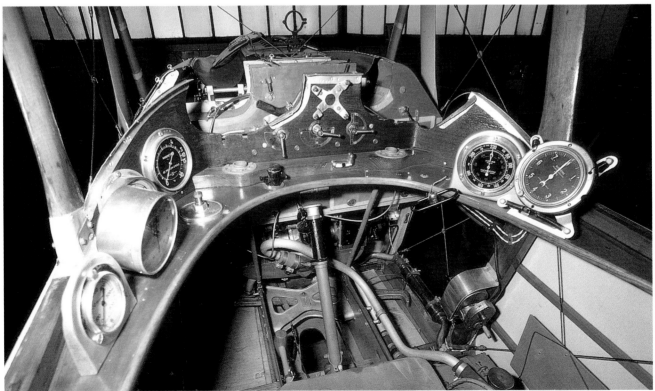

Above By June 1990 the SPAD was finished, and had been moved to La Ferté Alais from the old Memorial Flight workshop at Meudon. It was unable to fly at that year's airshow, however, since the paperwork had not been completed, but was parked in front of the hanger alongside the Flight's fully airworthy Fokker Dr.1 replica. The markings chosen represent those of Charles Henry Dolan, one of the American volunteers who flew with the *Escadrille Lafayette* before the United States entered the war

Right Alain Vallet, the Memorial Flight President, runs up the SPAD's Hispano. The tail is kept high for engine runs since the oil and water systems do not function very well with the aircraft in a tail down position. Clearly visible here are the shutters that control the amount of air through the radiator, the prominent bulges in the cowling that cover the cylinder heads and the fuel feed pipes from the upper wing gravity tank. Since its second 'first' flight in May 1991, this fighter has been the only airworthy original SPAD in the world – it is also one of the finest French aircraft restorations yet managed. Considerable work has gone into making the smallest details correct, and the paint scheme uses correctly pigmented varnish, rather than paint. It is flown very occasionally by either Alain Vallet or Jean Salis, without whose generosity it would have undoubtedly remained grounded

Above The Champlin Fighter Museum in Arizona has a collection of original and replica aircraft from both World Wars. Among them is this fine replica SPAD, completed in 1987. It was built by Dick Day of New Jersey and Herb Tischler of Fort Worth, Texas, and is painted to represent the machine flown by Lt Frank Luke, who was born and bred in Arizona. His family were present when this replica was dedicated to him soon after its completion

Above right Many of the Morane Saulnier Company's aircraft were fitted with the parasol wing configuration, the single flying surface being supported by struts above the fuselage. This gave excellent visibility downwards and also upwards since the pilots eyes were in line with the wing. Their last wartime design was the AI, known in service as the MoS XXVII or XXIX, depending on its armament, and two can be seen here, together with a postwar MoS 138 parasol-winged trainer powered by an 80 hp Le Rhône

Right Although the Morane Saulnier AI's time at the front was relatively short, partly as a result of it being powered by the temperamental 160 hp Gnôme, it became a successful training aeroplane when re-engined with the 130 hp Clerget. Several original examples survive, and the Salis Collection has one airworthy AI semi-replica. Three of these were originally constructed for a film, one later being sold and a third damaged when it overturned on landing during the 1992 La Ferté airshow after having hit craters formed during the making of another film!

Above left The collection at La Ferté Alais had originally been started by Jean Salis's father, Jean Baptiste Salis, prior to World War 2. Many of his original aircraft were dispersed by the Germans during the occupation, and the collection was started again after the war. Among the items found were three genuine Morane Saulnier AIs, two of which were disposed of abroad, whilst the third eventually went to the *Musée de l'Air*. In 1991 it was passed to the Memorial Flight Association for rebuilding to airworthy condition, which was duly completed in early 1993

Left The Memorial Flight AI is finished as an MoS XXIX – the twin-gun version – as operated by the Spa 160, complete with their Devil on a Broomstick Logo. The choice of this is significant since the squadron was eventually amalgamated with the *Escadrille Lafayette* and

Spa 3 *Les Cinognes*, or Storks, and now flies Mirage 2000s. In 1991 the Memorial Flight SPAD was guest of honour at the 75th anniversary celebrations of the *Escadrille Lafayette*, and the Morane consolidates that historical link that stretches back over seven decades

Above The Morane's cockpit shows its relatively limited forward view, as well as the sparse cockpit instrumentation of just an altimeter and a rev counter. To the right of the altimeter is the fuel pulsator, and in the centre is the tiny slip ball. Below these are the on/off switches for fuel and oil and the Bosche magneto switch. Just visible on the left-hand side are the fuel and air controls for the 130 hp Clerget. The cables leading from the control column operate the twin Vickers guns, whilst the map is a copy of an original from World War 1 and the rear view mirror reveals a camera!

Above The *Musée de l'Air*/Memorial Flight Morane AI now resides at La Ferté Alais along with the SPAD, Fokker Dr.1 replica and many other treasures. Despite its frail appearance, the Morane AI was very strong – the struts, which in this photo appear to be made of wood, are in fact steel tubing with wooden fairings. The Morane is more than capable of withstanding +8 and –4g, figures which are the equal of many fine aerobatic aircraft. In 1928 a Type 30, the postwar training variant, performed a world record 1111 consecutive loops, a figure which, unsurprisingly, still remains unbeaten!

Above right The Memorial Flight's Morane AI is normally flown by Roger Louis Texier, a former *Armée de l'Air* pilot who currently flies a commercial L-100

Hercules during the week. Like many pilots of World War 1 aeroplanes, he claims it is actually nicer to remember flying these aeroplanes over a beer than it is to actually do it. The Morane is fast and manoeuvrable, and can be quite a handful on take-off and landing

Right Another original Morane AI can be seen at Old Rheinbeck. This was one of a pair that were bought at the famous 'Wings and Wheels' auction at Orlando, Florida in 1981. It has since been totally rebuilt, as was its 160 hp Gnôme engine – this totally original powerplant gives the AI very challenging flying characteristics, particularly when one bears in mind the considerable power on offer from this massively impressive rotary, and the brain-numbing level of vibration it pushes through the airframe

Above This rear view of the Old Rheinbeck AI clearly shows the one-piece wing with its inset ailerons, and the elegant circular faired fuselage. The front fuselage is made up of a steel-tube frame, and the rear from a conventional wooden frame, braced with wire. The outside shape is then made up with stringers, tapering to a point at the tail. Unlike some earlier Morane Saulnier designs, the AI had separate elevators, rather than an 'all flying' tail

Right Operating World War 1 aeroplanes is not just a case of jumping in and taking off. There is a considerable work to be done on the ground, as engines and aircraft need careful preparation, and even moving them around on an airfield is not overly easy. The tail of the AI weighs about 150 kilos, and there is only room for one pair of hands on the tailcone, and nowhere else to hold on when moving it

USAEF

Since the end of World War 2 there has been a steady increase in the number of replica World War 1 aeroplane built, as well as original aircraft returned to the skies. There were a few people who attempted to preserve original aeroplanes in airworthy condition before 1939, both in Europe and in the United States, but these were few and far between. It is possible that in the new nuclear age some people began to look back on World War 1 as a cleaner, more chivalrous, war, making the comparison between early fliers and the knights of legend. Perhaps a small part of this romantic vision is true, but fighting, and dying, in the air in 1917 was just as nasty as in later years.

It is also possible that with the rapid development of jet aircraft, which became weapon systems rather than aeroplanes, some people began to look back at a time when everything was just that much simpler, or perhaps individuals simply wanted to find out what these aeroplanes were actually like to fly. It is one thing to see a static aeroplane in a museum, but it is altogether something else to hear the noise of its engine, see the vibration in its fabric and flying wires, smell the castor oil and experience the totally different control characteristics of those early aeroplanes, and to compare them with today's light aircraft, or even the fighters of a generation later.

It is also true to say that to build and operate a replica World War 1 fighter is far cheaper than operating a warbird from World War 2, although if one wants to make the replica as accurate as possible, or to operate an original aeroplane, this figure can climb dramatically to a point not too far distant from those combat aircraft of 25 years later.

Of the small number of original World War 1 aeroplanes still flying, most belong to the Shuttleworth Collection in England, the late Cole Palen's collection in New York State or the Memorial Flight Association near Paris. There are others in private hands, but many of these are now being retired into museums as they are too valuable to fly. This has led many people to build replicas. Some of these are built to exacting standards, and others are built to look and to fly in a way that is similar to the original aeroplane, but using different materials and later engines.

Rebuilding an original aeroplane is relatively straightforward providing that it is complete. Unfortunately, this is rarely the case, and it is fortunate that over the last 20 or 30 years considerable work has gone into locating as many original drawings as possible through organisations such as *World War One Aero* in the United States and *Cross and Cockade* in Britain, and

Above The Curtiss Jenny was to America what the Avro 504 was to Britain, and over 50 examples are known to have survived to this day, many of which are still airworthy, or currently being restored. One such example is owned by Ray Folsom of California, and has been restored in the same colours that it wore when at March Field in 1918. The Jenny, or Curtiss JN-4, was used to train most US pilots of World War 1, and a considerable number of British ones as well. Postwar, many Jennies were used for barnstorming, as their stability and rugged construction made climbing all over them whilst in flight a relatively easy task!

much time has been spent re-drawing and re-designing the original aircraft factory plans. One case in point is the Fokker Dr.1 Triplane. Original drawings for this do not exist, but in the 1960s an enthusiast called Walt Redfern decided that he would like to build one. He found that the Dr.1's designer, Rheinhold Platz, was still alive and living in Germany, so he contacted him. Platz was able to give a lot of information about the design, and this, together with contemporary writings and sketches, plus original photographs, was to prove the basis of the redesign. Redfern's plans are available for those who wish to build one for themselves, and many of the Dr.1s flying today are based on these drawings, or simliar ones available from Ron Sands . The design has been simplified a little to make life easier for amateur builders, but they can be used as a basis for a convincing replica, and with a little extra research work, such as that performed by Eberhard Fritsch in Germany, can produce an aircraft which is about as accurate as it is physically possible to get.

In some cases the original drawings exist, but are impossible to obtain. For example, the remaining store of Sopwith drawings are held by British Aerospace, who refuse to allow them to be used in the rebuilding or

Left While most JN-4s were powered by the Curtiss OX-5 engine, some were built to take the Hispano-Suiza of 150 hp. One example is now flown at Old Rheinbeck, having been acquired by Cole Palen in 1957 as a complete 'basket case'. Parts were collected over a long period from a variety of sources and restoration finally began in 1967. Completed just two years later, the Jenny is now finished in Olive Drab as '38278', and it has been a regular performer at the many shows held at Old Rheinbeck each year

Right Despite having an early lead in aviation, the United States were somewhat left behind by developments in France, Britain and Germany in the early years of World War 1. Consequently, most combat pilots of the USAAC flew foreign aircraft. In January 1917, the Thomas Morse Aircraft Corporation was formed, and their chief designer, B D Thomas (no relation to the founders), who had previously worked for Avro in England before helping to design the Curtiss Jenny, came up with a single-seat training aeroplane designated the S-4. This was designed around the 100 hp Gnôme, but most were fitted with the 80 hp Le Rhône, and they could be armed with a single machine gun. These aircraft served exclusively in the United States, and many found their way into private ownership after the Armistice

replicating of airworthy aircraft because of the possibility of product liability problems should a replica crash. This is understandable in today's highly bureaucratic world, but is nevertheless a crying shame since most people who wish to build replicas of this type of aeroplane fully appreciate their limitations and flying characteristics, and are not likely to try to sue a later manufacturer for the design of a 75-year-old aeroplane. It is also fortunate that most builders and flyers of these machines operate them well within their limits, and as a result accidents are thankfully very rare.

The main component on any aeroplane is its engine, and World War 1 powerplants are not widely avaiable, although they can sometimes be found, or traded from museums or collections. Many replicas, and almost all original aircraft, are fitted with the correct engines, but others are fitted with later types. To say that they are fitted with modern engines is somewhat misleading, as many of the powerplamts used, such as the Warner Scarab, have not been made since World War 2.

Besides the general availabilty of these later engines, there are two further reasons for fitting a more modern 'lump'. The first is that early engines, such as rotaries, have a very short overhaul life and need constant attention, which is both time-consuming and expensive, and flying time is consequently restricted as a result – it follows that if one has spent thousands of hours building a replica, flying for more than two or three hours per year would be preferable. The second reason is one of reliability. Elderly engines do not take kindly to long cross-country flights, so if the aeroplane is to be used at airshows, or for pleasure flying, a more reliable

engine will prevent unintentional returns to earth. AJD Engineering of Suffolk have designed a mounting to fit into an Avro 504 that will take either an original rotary engine or a static radial engine. The only changes to the airframe are four extra brackets behind the firewall. For airshow work and cross-country flying, the aeroplane can be fitted with a 145 hp Warner Scarab. If a rotary is to be fitted, the cowling and engine mount are changed, the fuel and oil drained and the engine plumbed in – the whole change takes just a few hours.

The operators of the few original aeroplanes that are still flying have no real choice but to fit period engines. Since the flying time on the airframe is limited, due both to its age and value, the engine does not have to operate for more than a few hours each year. For those pilots lucky enough to fly these aeroplanes goes the massive responsibility of keeping them in one piece.

Most early aeroplanes are relatively simple. Wings are generally made up with two load carrying spars, with wing ribs over these to give the airfoil shape. The fuselage is made up of frames attached to the longitudinal longerons, either in wood or in steel tube, and braced with wire. Wooden stringers make up the final shape and the whole lot is covered in fabric, usually Irish linen or cotton. Whilst these parts are usually relatively easy to manufacture, the multitude of metal fittings that hold them together and

Above Of the many Thomas Morse Scouts to survive, only one now remains airworthy. This was bought as a virtual wreck from veteran film pilot Paul Mantz in 1955 by Ernest Freeman. Restoration took 17 years, with Freeman's son Roger helping out, and he is now the Scout's sole pilot. Much of the structure of the aeroplane had to be replaced during the rebuild, but great care went into remanufacturing the pieces correctly. The major find was a completely unused 80 hp Le Rhône, still wrapped in 1918 newspapers, that was discovered in a San Antonio boatyard! The Scout now wears the same markings it wore in 1918

Right The final Nieuport fighter of World War 1 was the Type 28.C1, which was used by several American fighter units in France during 1918. Unlike earlier Nieuport biplanes, the upper and lower wings were of the same chord, and since the lower wing had two spars rather than one, it featured normal interplane struts rather than V-shaped ones. This example, rebuilt by Skysport Engineering, was acquired from the Wings and Wheels auction in Orlando on behalf of Aero Vintage Ltd, and flew again in 1991 powered by the incredibly noisy 160 hp Le Rhône

attach each part to its neighbour can be extremely time consuming to make. This is especially the case on an all-wooden aeroplane like a Sopwith Pup, where the fuselage is held together entirely by its bracing wires. These wires are attached to brackets that hold the vertical and horizontal members by a system of clips, bolts and brackets in a variety of sizes and styles. To build a Pup, or indeed any of Sopwith's aeroplanes, which all use the same system, requires a considerable amount of sheet metal work.

Of course not all aircraft are built that way. One reason the Fokker Dr.1 is so popular is that the welded steel fuselage is quite straightforward to build. The only problem with the Fokker is one of space, since the wings have single spars that are full span. Eberhard Fristch tells the story of how he moved his wife out of their bedroom since it was the only room in the house which had enough room to allow him to make the seven-metre long spars. She said later that she thought about leaving him, but decided that if she did she would still have to find another bedroom!

Once the project is completed, be it a replica or an original, there will come a time when it will fly. Most people who build or rebuild World War 1 aeroplanes wish to experience at first-hand the flying characteristics of these old machines. For pilots used to flying modern light aircraft World War 1 machines can come as quite a shock. Fighters from any period are not designed for pleasure flying – they are designed to enable the pilot to fire at another aircraft. This is certainly the case in World War 1 aeroplanes, and their functional design is further compounded by their primitive aerodynamics, and the type of engines used.

Rotary engines in particular create an enormous amount of torque which tries to turn the aeroplane in the opposite direction to the propeller. It has been said that it is just as easy to turn a Sopwith Camel, or a Triplane, through 270° to the left as it is to turn it 90° to the right. The only instruction for take-off in the pilots notes for the Morane AI is to apply full left rudder, accompanied by full power. This would not have been a problem during World War 1 since most, if not all, airfields were simply large areas of grass, and take-off could always be directly into the wind. In these days of set runways, crosswinds are more of a problem, and Roger Louis Texier of the Memorial Flight says of the Morane that, 'It is best to keep the tail down in the early part of the run until there is enough speed for the rudder to become effective. The aeroplane is always trying to swing and the skid digging into the ground helps a lot. I would not like to take-off as it says in the book, as you would never know in which direction you would end up'.

Most pilots of World War 1 aeroplanes agree that estimates of the power of some of the engines are far too low, and this, combined with the gyroscopic action of the rotary engines, can lead to some very interesting experiences. Stuart Goldspink, who flew the Aero Vintage Nieuport 28 and the AJD Engineering Sopwith Camel states that, 'The 160 Gnôme on the Nieuport was definitely far more powerful than a mere 160 horsepower. On take-off the aeroplane would virtually be on one wheel and you needed considerable aileron to keep the wing up. In flight any increase in power would kick the aeroplane around, and if a lot of power was applied it would almost go onto one wingtip'.

The control of rotary engines can also give some headaches, especially the system used on the Nieuport 28. Some people who flew Nieuport 28s after the war reverted to a standard throttle, but the rebuild by Skysport Engineering of the Aero Vintage example used the original switch system. Stuart Goldspink explained, 'On full power settings and slightly reduced

Right The Aero Vintage Nieuport 28 was one of several that featured in the Hollywood films of the 1930s, including *Wings* and both versions of *Dawn Patrol.* Indeed, a photograph exists of this very aeroplane with Errol Flynn in the cockpit. At some stage in its history the wings were clipped to improve turning performance in pylon racing, and by the time it was acquired in 1981 it was in a sorry state. A considerable amount of research went into the rebuild to make it as accurate as possible, and it was eventually finished in the colours of the 94th Aero Squadron. Sadly, this beast of a machine flies no more, having been traded to an American museum

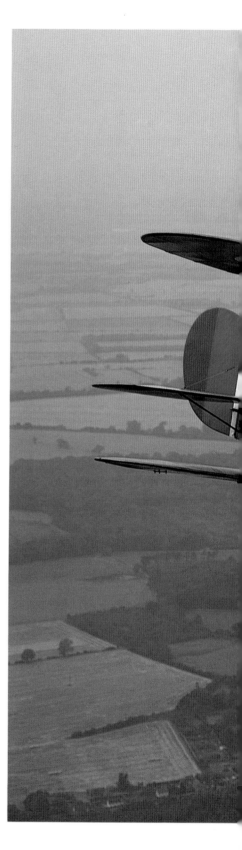

power it was not too bad, but if a low power setting was used while airborne the top wings seemed to want to hit the lower wings, there was so much vibration. I could understand why Jean Salis in France told us it would eventually shake itself to pieces, and that we should fit a normal throttle, but at full power it was very fast'.

Goldspink's impression of the Camel is somewhat different. 'I liked the Camel, although I only flew it for about an hour-and-a-half before it was sold, but I enjoyed it. It was not as fierce as I had expected. Whether this was because we had a 110 hp Le Rhône in it and not a 130 hp Clerget or a 150 hp Bentley I am not sure? It swung on take-off, but not too much, and was, like most World War 1 aeroplanes, tail heavy in the air and needed constant attention. I found that it was like the Sopwith Dove and Pup, and had insufficient rudder and fin area, but it was the fastest pitching aeroplane I have ever known. A change in power and the nose would go up or down very quickly. I did not get the chance to do aerobatics in it. It would have looped very easily, but rolls would have been difficult because the ailerons were not very good; the Nieuport was the same in this respect.'

The ailerons on most of these aeroplane are not balanced, so when the aileron goes down to increase the lift and raise the wing, the drag causes the wing to lose lift, and the aircraft to yaw.

The SPAD, too, can be interesting. Alain Vallet of the Memorial Flight occasionally flies it and says, 'It is very fast and very powerful. The ailerons are very stiff and it takes some effort to get it into a turn, and once there it will continue forever if you let it. As it also takes quite a bit of effort to get it out of the turn, it would not be too good in a dogfight. It would stand no chance angainst a D.VII or a Triplane. It is far better as an attack aircraft, as it is strong enough to be dived at up to 450 kmph, which is over 280 mph, and could be used in combat in the same way as the P-47 Thunderbolt was in World War 2. Both could be dived onto their prey, and they would climb out after the attack using the speed that had built up in the dive, ready for another go. The SPAD also lands fast because of its thin wing. It has to be brought in with power, but once the power is cut it does not float but drops onto the runway. Jean Salis says flying the SPAD is like flying the Grumman Bearcat.'

Whislt most Fokker Triplane replicas are powered with radial or flat-four engines, there are a few people fortunate enough to have flown them with rotary engines. Gerard Leclerc of the Memorial Flight is one, and his impressions of the Fokker are that once the tail is up on the take-off run, directional control is quite easy, whereas with the tail down it is not too good. The take-off run is very short, and the aeroplane climbs very well. He added, 'Once in the air I did not find it too tail heavy, which has been said about the aeroplane, but it is directionally very unstable since there is no fixed fin area to help. The ailerons are balanced and are very light, but

Below Despite the fact that very few original drawings exist of the Nieuport 28, a number of replicas have been made over the years, powered by engines ranging from Warner Scarabs to 220 hp Continentals. The plans problem was overcome by redesigning the airframe to use modern materials. This Type 28 replica was built by Jim Robertson and Harry Wooldridge, and differs from the original in having a welded-steel tube fuselage, redesigned wings and Ceconite airframe covering

Above Pictured above Lake Guntersville, Alabama, during the *Aerodrome '92* airshow (the first of what is set to become an annual event which features only World War 1 aeroplanes and replicas) is the Robertson/Wooldridge Nieuport 28 replica. This aeroplane now belongs to Frank Ryder's Replica Fighter Museum at the nearby Guntersville airport, where it is flown more frequently than would be the case if it were an original

not very effective – you can push the stick from one side to the other without it affecting your flight too much. Turning right is easier than turning left, and a considerable amount of opposite rudder is needed in the turn'. With regard to the Triplane's gliding performance, Leclerc agreed with Robin Bowes, who once described his Triplane as having the same glide angle as a piano.

Another man who has considerable experience with old aeroplanes is replica builder Vivien Bellamy. He has built a 130 hp Clerget-engined Camel and described how it needed full left rudder whichever way it turned. 'One way the nose went up and you had to kick it down with the rudder, and the other way it dropped and you needed to haul it up.' Bellamy is also of the opinion that most World War 1 aeroplanes are more powerful and faster than they have ever been given credit for, but he did raise a very interesting point. 'I flew Cole Palen's rotary-engined Fokker Dr.1 many years ago and that was powered by a 100 hp Gnôme. I flew my Camel several years later, but I would like to fly them both on the same day to make a proper comparison. I feel sure that there is almost nothing to choose between them, and in a fight, the victory would go to the more

Right The USAAC used the Nieuport 28 until they were replaced with SPAD XIIIs. The 1st Pursuit Group, however, held on to their Nieuports until after all other groups had changed to SPADs. By adapting and modifying the engines, the warm up time for the powerplant was significantly reduced, and the squadron could be airborne in 90 seconds from the time of an alert

Left The clean lines of the Nieuport 28 replica are evident here as it banks towards Howard Levy's camership. The late Cole Palen described his original Nieuport 28 as the perfect airshow aeroplane since it was fast, looked good and it was loud and whilst few aeroplanes, even some jets, are as loud as a 160 hp Gnôme, these replicas still look elegant and purposeful. Since both the Aero Vintage and Palen Nieuport 28s are now retired, the only way you will get to see one of these machines aloft is by watching a replica

experienced pilot, or the one who had the element of surprise.'

With regard to fighting in these aeroplane, Stuart Goldspink said that with all of the rotary-engined aeroplanes he has flown, he has been virtually blind after no more than a few minutes aloft because of the stream of unburnt Castor Oil that flies everywhere, and covers the face and goggles with a thin black film. He said, 'I hate to think what it must have been like for the guys in the First World War', and so perhaps the final word should be about them.

The pilots of World War 1 were, on average, in their early twenties, although some were younger. James McCudden was just 22 when he died in July 1918, and Manfred von Richthofen only 25. They had to fly these aeroplanes, which today are treated so kindly, to the limits in bad weather up to heights of over 20,000 ft without oxygen, wearing just a layer of Goose grease to protect them from frostbite. Many pilots sat on, or next to, fuel tanks that were unarmoured and pressurised so that a single shot could incinerate them. They were not allowed parachutes to enable them to have a chance of life should this happen, and many chose to fall to their deaths rather than burn. Others took their service revolver with them to hasten the end in the event of a fire

At certain times during the ever changing balance of power, pilots of either side could count their life expectancy in days rather than years or even weeks. Ground attack and trench strafing was carried out at altitudes so low that a German Officer was reportedly run down by an S.E.5a. The return fire was great enough to convince some pilots that they should sit on their standard issue tin hats since the fabric of a Camel, or an S.E.5a, offered no protection whatsoever against a hail of lead. Young men fresh out of training squadrons would be sent into battle with fewer hours than is now required to complete a Private Pilots Licence. Many of these did not even see the aeroplane and man that shot them down. Some that did survive drank to forget the fear, and all that came home told of recurring nightmares of burning aircraft and of falling through the sky.

Of those survivors there are now fewer and fewer each year as old age finally gathers them up. In a few years none will be left to give their own accounts of what it was like to fly and fight in aircraft little different to a Tiger Moth. There will, however, be a good number of original and replica aeroplanes that will fly to remind us all of their bravery, whatever side they were on, and to give some of us a chance to experience the smell of burnt Castor Oil and the rattle of old engines.

Right The USAAC also used the Sopwith Camel. This replica was built by AJD Engineering for the Fort Rucker Army Museum in Alabama, and contains many original parts. It is finished in the colours of a machine flown by Lt Henry R 'Hank' Clay Jnr of the 41st Aero Pursuit Squadron, who were based in France during 1918. The replica is seen temporarily fitted with an 80 hp Le Rhône engine, although a 130 hp Clerget was eventually supplied to the museum

Idflieg

Left Discovered in a barn as late as the 1970s, the Champlin Fighter Museum's Aviatik (Berg) D.I is one of only two in the world. It was designed by Julius von Berg in 1917 and, due to its simple construction, was built by several subcontractors. The powerplant was the 200 hp Austro Diamler engine, and most were armed with twin synchronised machine guns. When found, the D.I had a 100 hp Gnôme engine attached, plus an extra seat added in front of the original cockpit, possibly to disguise it as a civilian type in order to avoid it being confiscated by the Allies, who rounded up all military aeroplanes in Austro-Hungary postwar and scrapped them. It has since been restored to its former glory, complete with its correct engine and guns

Above Only one original Fokker E.III exists, and that is suspended from the roof of the Science Museum in London. It was delivered almost brand new into the hands of the Allies on 8 April 1916 after its delivery pilot got lost over the Western Front near Valenciennes. Several replicas have been built over the years, and one of the first of these was constructed by Personal Plane Services, which has since been used in a number of films. It was originally going to have the correct warped wings, all flying tail and a rotary engine, but due to the amount of use it was likely to see, its builders decided to fit conventional elevators, a Continental C85 and adapted Tiger Moth wings, complete with elevators. It is seen here in 1970 over the Buckinghamshire countryside with former P-47 pilot, Bill Evans, at the controls

Above The Albatros company did not just make fighters, but had a reputation for building successful reconaissance aircraft too. Very few of these have survived, and so when such aircraft are needed for film work there is no alternative but to adapt whatever is available. One aircraft type that has, over the years, 'fought' on both sides is the Tiger Moth. The Salis Collection has two Albatross C.II lookalikes built up from Tiger Moth parts, with upright engines, no top decking and new tails. The main giveaway when looking at these is the fact the pilot sits in the observer's cockpit, facing forward

Above right One of the rarer types to be found at the front was the Halberstadt D.IV. The company had built a number of successful two-seat reconnaissance aircraft and light bombers, but few fighters, and these only served in combat for a limited time in late 1916 and early 1917. None of these have survived, and prolific replica builder

Carl Swanson, of Wisconsin, had only a three-view drawing and a single photo on which to base this replica, which first flew in 1983. The original Halberstadts were powered by a 120 hp Argus, but due to the obvious rarity of such an engine, the replica has a 150 hp ENMA Super Tigre fitted instead, which is usually found bolted to a Spanish-built Bücker Jüngmann

Right Like many of the replicas built in the USA, the Halberstadt differs from the original in having a steel-tube fuselage (although in this case it is covered in plywood), brakes and a tailwheel for flying from hard runways, which are the norm in America. This aeroplane was originally painted in a primarily green scheme and known as *Die Grosse Zuchinni*, but it has since moved to the Frank Ryder Replica Fighter Museum, where it has been repainted in this slightly more representative scheme

Above The late Cole Palen's contribution to World War 1 preservation and replica building cannot be overestimated. Many of the aircraft flown at Old Rheinbeck were as faithful to the originals as possible. One such example was his Albatross D.Va, built in the late 1960s. This was fitted with an original Mercedes engine (although this has subsequently had to be replaced by a Ranger), original instruments, and it even looked like an original aeroplane. Clearly visible in this photograph is the externally mounted RPM indicator

Right Virtually all D.Vas suffered structural failures whilst diving, these being caused by flutter in the lower wing, a phenomenon not fully understood at the time. The answer was to fit extra bracing, and this can be seen ahead of the V-strut, attached to the lower wing. Other than this minor problem(!), the D.Va was a fine aeroplane, although not as nice to fly as its precessor the D.III. Only two D.Vas survive today, one in the Australian War Museum in Canberra and the other in the National Air and Space Museum in Washington DC

Above Another of Leisure Sport's replicas was this D.Va built in Germany by Art Williams. It was powered by an air-cooled Ranger engine which is normally run inverted, but has been converted to run upright. The differences in weight made this aeroplane tail heavy, something that is quite common with World War 1 replicas, and it was not overly popular with the collection's pilots. It has subsequently been sold to the Fleet Air Arm museum in Yeovilton, Somerset, and has not flown for some time, although work has recently been carried out to improve its aerodynamics

Above right Walt Redfern is best known as the man who produced the first plans for the Fokker Dr.1, but he has also built other replicas inlcuding a D.H.2 and this Albatross D.Va, constructed with the assistance of the late Bob Sleep. This fighter is powered by the ubiquitous 200 hp Ranger engine and was completed in July 1990. The drawings used were those prepared by the Smithsonian after the rebuild of their genuine D.Va, and construction is the same as the original, although the replica weighs in slightly lighter, partly due to it having an air-cooled, rather than water-cooled, engine. This aeroplane is now resident in Guntersville, Alabama, along with no less than 33 other replica and semi-scale aircraft that form Frank Ryder's Replica Fighter Museum

Right The cockpit of the Redfern/Sleep D.Va shows the original style control grip and the wooden frames that hold the separately formed plywood fuselage sides together. Non-standard items include more modern instruments, included for ease of flying rather than historical accuracy, the British compass and the radio, but the general layout follows that of the original Albatros

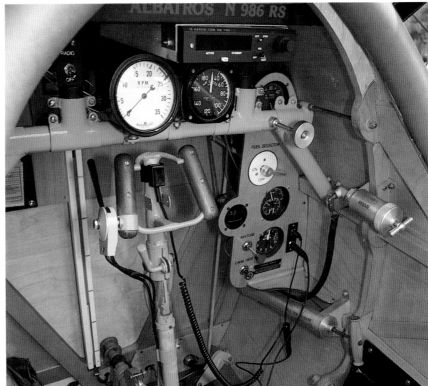

Left Undoubtedly the most readily identifiable World War 1 aeroplane is the Fokker Dr.1, and although rumours persist, there are no originals in existence anywhere in the world. There are, however, many replicas, some better than others, and one of the best is that flown by the Memorial Flight. It was started in Germany by Eberhard Fritsch, who subsequently joined the association and moved the almost complete aircraft to Paris to unite it with a rotary engine. In this photo of the aeroplane under trial assembly, the thick double box spars which gave the wing their strength can be seen, along with the welded-tube fuselage, a Fokker trademark

Above Considerable research has gone into producing the most accurate replica possible. Ron Sands' plans were used as a basis for the general construction of the Dr.I, and research was also carried out in the Fokker archives, the *Musée de l'Air* and by *Cross and Cockade* in the UK. All instrumentation is original, including the compass that, unfortunately, was later stolen from the aeroplane whilst parked at Le Ferté Alais a few years ago. The only non-standard items are the lozenge fabric behind the seat and wrapping over the longerons, this being used primarily because that was all that was available at the *Musée de l'Air* at the time

Above Alain Vallet, the Memorial Flight President, is seen here in the cockpit after another succesful engine run. The guns fitted to the Triplane are originals on loan from the *Musée de l'Air*. They were donated to the museum by the French ace Madon, who had removed them from an aircraft he had shot down. Also visible is the Aldis telescopic sight and the lack of bracing wires, apart fom those on the centre-section struts

Left Portrait of a happy aircraft builder. Eberhard Fritsch relaxes with a beer (German, of course) after the display at La Ferté in 1993. Regardless of how short the flight, there is considerable work to done after landing to clean off the Castor Oil that is liberally sprayed out by the 160 hp Le Rhône engine, and a beer is always welcome after such labours. Since building the Fokker, Fritsch has completed a Blériot XI-2 *Militaire* and started work on a Fokker D.VIII, as well as restoring parts of the Memorial Flight's Avro 504 and LVG. Future projects include a Fokker E.III, an Albatross D.Va a Fokker D.VII and perhaps a Caproni bomber! Eberhard Fritsch does not watch much television

Above No mocked-up metal tubing or fibreglass moulding in the shape the Dr.I's deadly twin Spandau 7.92 mm machine guns for the Memorial Flight's Triplane replica – these are, as previously mentioned, the 'genuine article'. Like the British Lewis and Vickers guns, the Spandau was the staple weapon fitted to virtually all German combat aircraft of World War 1

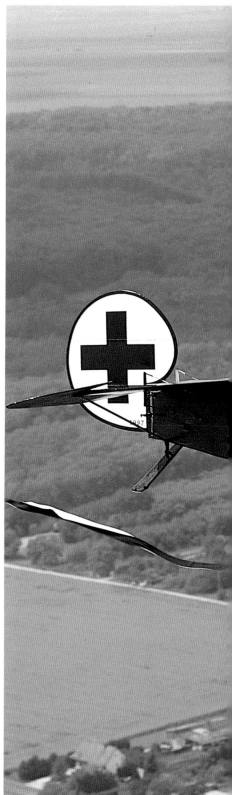

Above Although the original Dr.1s were powered by a 110 hp Oberursel rotary, the Memorial Flight replica is powered by a 160 hp Le Rhône. This is a development of the 110 hp Le Rhône, of whch the Oberursel was a copy, and this particular engine was used in an experimental helicopter in 1920, before being acquired by the *Musée de l'Air*. The non-standard cutouts on the front of the cowling were applied to some original Triplanes to ease engine cooling. The fighter is finished in the markings of Karl Bölle, commander of the Boelke *Jasta*. Eberhard Fritsch is reported to have said, 'I don't care what colour you paint it as long as it is not red', referring to the all too common practice of painting aircraft to represent those of Manfred von Richthofen

Right Pictured above the French countryside is Christian Ravel in the Memorial Flight Dr.1. Ravel is a hugely experienced pilot, his normal day job being to fly the Boeing 747-400, but he is also an accomplished glider pilot, flying instructor and President of the *Groupement pour la Préservation du Patrimoine Aéronautique* at Angers. He lists the Dr.1 among his favourites out of the 200+ aircraft and 150 gliders he has flown during the 17,000 hours accumulated in his logbook

Above Another French Triplane replica is that of the Jean Salis collection. This has been used in a number of films, and is powered by a Warner Scarab radial engine. Many Triplane replicas are powered by Scarabs since they are one of the few radial engines that will fit into a rotary cowling, even though they are a little longer

Right In some of the early Hollywood epics, such as *Wings*, the actors playing the leading roles had to be able to fly their own aircraft, and cockpit shots were actually filmed whilst on the wing! Today this is rarely the case due to the expense of flying these machines, and it is far better to place the aircraft on a rig, with the engine running, and have the pilot pretend to fly. Such work is often carried out at La Ferté Alais, where their Fokker, complete with the markings of von Richthofen's last aircraft, can be seen performing here for a TV series

Above For many years there was only one Fokker Dr.1 replica in the United Kingdom. Built from Redfern plans by Vivien Bellamy for the Leisure Sport company, it was bought by Robin Bowes, who has regularly displayed it all over the country. This too is powered by a 145 hp Warner Scarab, but from a distance, as it turns over the trees at Old Warden, the home of the Shuttleworth Collection, it could be mistaken for the real thing. This aeroplane is now flying again after an accident in 1992 that saw it perform a forced landing on a football field in Dusseldorf – it ended up on its back. Bowes was unhurt, but the looks on the faces of the firemen as they arrived to find a World War 1 fighter in the colours of their most famous ace were something to behold

Right Unlike the Memorial Flight aeroplane, not all Triplanes have a period cockpit fit. This American-registered example, now resident in France, has a moden array of instruments and several other non-standard features such as a different control column and brakes

Above Robin Bowes banks his Triplane past the crowd at Old Warden during a display in May 1992. This machine has carried the markings of two of Richthofen's Triplanes, but is seen here masquerading as 425/17, the Dr.1 in which Ricthofen met his death. In the first year after buying the replica, Robin Bowes flew more hours than Richthofen managed in his entire career as he ferried the Triplane between airshows where he would, almost inevitably, get 'shot down'

Left Like the Camel, the Triplane had most of its major weights close to the centre of gravity, and a boasted a short fuselage and short-span wings, which made it very manoeuvrable. The thick airfoil section on the wings also gave it a good rate of climb, but on landing these would block out the forward view rather like a set of Venetian blinds. As with all World War 1 aeroplanes, it has to be flown all the time, and cannot be left to its own devices. It is also tricky to handle on the ground, especially in a crosswind

Left Another machine built from the Ron Sands drawings is owned and flown by Fred Murrin of Pennsylvania. He built the Triplane over a period of nine years and tried hard to make it as authentic as possible, although he has had to fit a 150 hp Lycoming engine due to the problems of finding and operating original rotaries. This is finished in the colours of the pre-production machine that was given to Manfred von Richthofen, hence the designation F.1 ahead of the serial number rather than Dr.1. Of the first three Triplanes, one was used for testing at Fokker's Schwerin works, one went to Richthofen and the third to Werner Voss

115

Above Another spurious scheme is found on Jim Appleby's Warner-engined Fokker Dr.1, seen here at Chino, California. This carries the seial of 151/17, has the frowning face on the cowling as used by Werner Voss and is finished in colours never seen on an original Dr.1. Visible in this view are the wing tip skids that are used to protect the wings should the aeroplane ground loop, and the interplane struts that are not load bearing as in most aircraft, but simply stop the wings from moving about too much in flight

Left The Fokker Triplane is undoubtedly the most popular of all World War 1 aeroplanes for the replica builder. There were only 320 original examples built, but the number of replicas flying worldwide must now be a healthy proportion of that number. Some of these are finsihed in authentic schemes, but many more are finished in colours that just make them look good. One such example is Chuck Wentworth's replica, seen here being flown by its builder for Frank Mormillo's camera

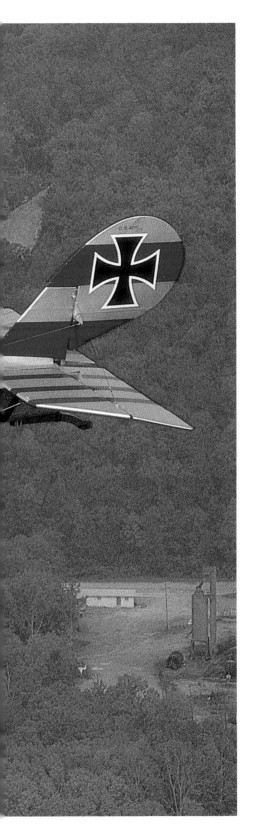

Above No less than four examples of the Pfalz D.XII have survived into the 1990s, primarily because the type found a home in the epic films of the 1930s, but no original example of the Pfalz D.III is known. For the film *The Blue Max*, which starred the late George Peppard, a number of Pfalz D.III replicas were built by Personal Plane Services. These were based on the Tiger Moth, although the similarity is not immediately apparent. New wings and tail assemblies were built, and the aircraft were originally fitted with Gypsy Major engines converted to run in the upright position – after the film was completed over two decades ago these replicas were placed in storage. However, they were recently purchased by Frank Ryder for his Alabama museum, and one of them was sold on to Javier Arango, who has rebuilt it with a 200 hp six-cylinder Gypsy Queen engine and painted it up in the colours of Lt Fritz Holn of *Jasta* 21

Left The Pfalz D.III first flew in the spring of 1917. It was similar in some respects to the Albatros since it had a semi-monocoque plywood fuselage and either a 160 hp or 180 hp Mercedes engine and, although it never received the acclaim of the Albatros or Fokker fighters, it was an effective aeroplane. Javier Arango acquired the Pfalz replica in early 1992, and had it rebuilt in time to appear at the *Aerodrome '92* meeting in Guntersville later that year. He reports that it is generally nice to fly although, in common with many World War 1 aeroplanes, it is heavy on the ailerons, so does not like rolling, and it is not overly stable

Above The LVG C.VI was developed from the earlier C.V as a two-seat reconnaissance and artillery observation aircraft. It was powered by the 200 hp Benz engine and about 1100 were built, of which just three survive. The most famous of these is that owned and flown by the Shuttleworth Collection. 7198/17 was forced down on 2 August 1918 by two S.E.5a pilots of No 74 Sqn, and was eventually exhibited as part of a charity drive in London. It was rebuilt to fly, and in 1937 appeared in the RAF Hendon Pageant, flying mock dogfights with a Sopwith Triplane, S.E.5a and a Bristol Fighter. It was acquired by the Shuttleworth Collection in 1959 and has since been rebuilt, thus making it the only genuine World War 1 two-seater currently airworthy anywhere in the world

Right Typifying the problems facing the operators of World War 1 aeroplanes, the radiator for the LVG was missing when it arrived at Old Warden. In order to get the aeroplane flying again, a radiator from a Renault car is now fitted, but the engine is still prone to overheating. One pilot of the LVG has said that his flight kit includes a teabag so that when the engine overheats and forces him down he can at least use some of the boiling water from the radiator to make himself a brew. Of the other two surviving LVG C.VIs, one is on display in the Brussels Air Museum and the other is under restoration by the Memorial Flight Association on behalf of the *Musée de l'Air*. The opportunity is also being taken to copy the latter aeroplane during its rebuilding so a replica, powered by an original Benz engine, will emerge from the workshops at Dugny in due course

Above The Fokker D.VII was undoubtedly one of the finest aircraft of World War 1, and some would go as far as to say it was the best. When it first appeared in early 1918, it was an immediate success. It was strong, fast and manoeuvrable, and it has been said that a D.VII could turn a mediocre pilot into a good one. Several original aircraft have survived, but none of these are now flying, although a good number of authentic replicas have been made. One such example was built by Arthur Williams in Germany, and was operated for some time by Leisure Sport in England. This machine was finished in the markings of Ernst Udet, an ace with Richthofen's *Jasta* 11, when went on to achieve a certain amount of fame during World War 2

Left Despite its occasional cooling problems the LVG frequently performs at the shows held at Old Warden, where it can usually be seen in mock combat with one of the collection's Allied fighters. Dave Davies's photograph sees it flying over the Bedfordshire countryside piloted by Desmond Penrose, and with Chief Engineer Chris Morris in the gunner's position. This view also shows the lozenge camouflage used by the Germans to good effect. Sadly, it proved too expensive to have this produced for the LVG, so the team at Old Warden are faced with hand painting each lozenge onto the fabric every time the wings are recovered!

Above The Fokker D.VII was unique in that it was the only aircraft referred to by name in the Armistice agreement. The Allies appreciated the D.VII for the fine aeroplane it was, and all machines, 'specifically those of the D.VII type' were required to be handed over. Fokker smuggled a large number across the border to his native Holland, where he rebuilt his business, but many originals found their way to the United States, and some were taken on strength by the Army Air Service. Others found their way to Hollywood to be used in such films as *Wings* and *Hell's Angels*. One of the few aircraft cited as being as good as the D.VII was the S.E.5a, and Javier Arango has replicas of both. His D.VII is seen here in formation with his 200 hp Lycoming-powered S.E.5a replica

Left Among the aircraft built for the film *Blue Max* were a number of Fokker D.VIIs. Unlike many replicas, which are powered by the Ranger engine of 200 hp converted to run upright rather than inverted, these were powered by 200 hp de Havilland Gypsy Queen engines which were used inverted, thus giving the nose countours of the D.VII an unusual shape. Following the filming many of the replicas remained in Ireland, until bought by Frank Ryder. One of these was sold to avid collector Javier Arango, who converted the engine to run upright, thereby reinstating its correct nose contours

Left Fokker's last design of the war was a parasol-winged monoplane powered by the Oberursel rotary of 110 hp. Despite its limited power, the design of the new fighter was quite advanced. The fuselage was the usual welded steel tube construction, and was very similar to the Dr.1, but the wing itself was a strong and efficient plywood-covered design, with inset ailerons. The D.VIII was aerodynamically clean, so Fokker was able to get as much performance from the 110 hp engine as other designers were getting from larger powerplants. Very few D.VIIIs reached the front primarily because the type was grounded for a while due to structural failures caused by Fokker's infamous lack of quality control

Overleaf By the time the wing problems were rectified the war was almost over and the D.VIII saw little action. The only surviving original parts from one of these fine fighters are a fuselage and engine held by the Caproni Museum in Italy. Few drawings of the D.VIII exist, so replica builders have been required to redesign the wing. A number of replicas have been constructed, like this radial-engined example kept by Frank Ryder's museum in Alabama, and more are in the pipeline, including one with a rotary engine which is to be built in Germany by Eberhard Fritsch